Contents

Introduction

Here's what you and your fellow teachers have been asking for — a collection of top-notch teaching ideas to help you add sparkle and innovation to your curriculum. All the ideas in this book have been taken from the pages of *Instructor* magazine and are teacher tested, guaranteed to be workable and successful. For just-starting-out teachers, they will be brand new. For experienced teachers, some may be reminders of those they once used but have since forgotten.

Unlike many idea books that try to be everything to everybody, this book has one emphasis — the basic subjects. Its ideas will enhance your teaching of reading, spelling, handwriting, math, social studies, science, health, physical education, art, music and more. A special chapter on learning activities across the curriculum will be especially useful.

Some of the ideas here are structured for whole-class use, some are best used with small groups, some are planned to help an individual child who has a special problem or a gifted pupil who needs a more challenging activity.

Read, or at least skim, the entire book first, noting those ideas you will use right away. Then read it again more carefully, a chapter at a time, noticing how the ideas can be linked to your curriculum. Earmark those that can be used later in the year, or when a pupil has a special need. You will find that the more you read, the more ways you will find to use and extend these top-notch ideas and suggestions.

READ AND ENJOY!

Reading and Literature

Introduction

Basal, phonics-centered, whole language—no matter what system of reading instruction your school uses or how complete it is, you always need a new idea to reinforce a special point. Here you'll find a way to help pupils understand blends, to encourage a child to read aloud more fluently, to promote interest in library books, to teach a main idea or point of view.

Play Ball!

Try this simple game for beginning readers. Write the same list of sight words on opposite sides of a file folder so two pupils can use it at once. Now make two baseball gloves, cutting a window in each and fitting the gloves over the folder so the words can be seen through the windows. Print the words again on small cards. To play, a "pitcher" reads the word on a card, and the two "catchers" each try to be the first to show the word in the window of his or her mitt.
BEVERLY YOUNG

Parent Reading Tips

Make this the year to actively involve parents in working with beginning readers. Send home a list of your favorite books for parents to read with their kids. You might want to suggest additional reading-related activities such as choosing a recipe to make, reading and following the directions together, and sharing the results. Send home helpful hints throughout the year to keep that parent-child partnership in reading going strong.
LYNN MINDERMAN

Vocabulary Building

One Rotten Apple

Build vocabulary skills with this interactive bulletin-board activity. Post a large cutout apple tree on the bulletin board, complete with a dozen or more large, removable construction-paper apples. At either side of the tree, place two cutout barrels. Label one barrel, "Good Apples," the other, "Rotten Apples." On half of the apples, write positive adjectives; on the other half, write negative ones. (Make sure you choose adjectives that are unfamiliar to most students.) Then, after students have found the definitions of the vocabulary, have each student "pick" an apple from the tree, read the word to the class, give its definition, and place it in the appropriate barrel. SANDRA J. FREY

Word Swap

This vocabulary expander puts new vocabulary words into active use.

Throughout the day, teachers use many routine phrases, such as "Line up," "Let's go to lunch." Try substituting the usual sentences with less common ones, such as "Let's go dine," "You may depart," "Stop the conversation," or "Align yourselves." Start with one or two phrases a week and use until the class masters them.

Help students pick new words for old standbys. Introduce the concept of synonyms and show them how to use the thesaurus.

As you think of new words to challenge your class, jot them down in a notebook and keep it on your desk as a reminder to use them.

JAN CHILDS

Wheel Of Words

Try this team activity for a fun vocabulary review. First, divide the class into teams of six. On the chalkboard, draw large wheels—one for each team. Next, draw spokes to divide each wheel into six parts. In the center of each wheel, write a word from a recent story or science unit, so that each team has the same word. To play, kids work as a team to write synonyms or antonyms for the word in the center. The round ends when the first team completes its wheel. Award all teams one point for each correct synonym or antonym and continue playing, placing new words in the center of each team's wheel. TIMOTHY HORNBERGER

Consonant Blend Snake

This curvy animal snakes around your classroom to encourage practice in reading skills. Build the snake with oaktag. Mount papers with the blends of the day on his middle and have students match word cards with the proper blend. SHARON KARLIN

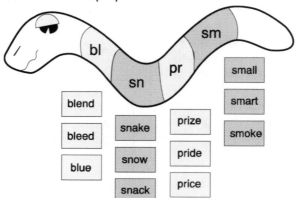

Vocabulary Building

Phonics Quenchers

Reinforce phonics lessons on initial consonant blends with this activity. Write two initial blends on each straw as shown. Then write an ending for each pair on a "glass," to yield a whole word. Ask kids to match, cut, and paste the straws to the glasses to make rhyming words.   LISA WATERS

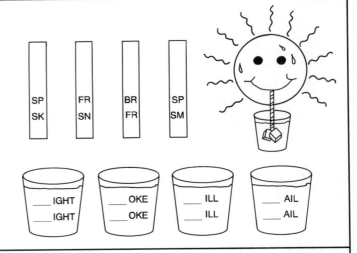

Word Posters

After presenting vocabulary words, assign one word from the list to each student. Ask each child to design a poster for his or her word showing the word written in large letters, its phonetic spelling, its definition, and a sentence containing it. Posters may also include drawings or pictures cut from magazines to illustrate the word's meaning. Then, to increase the word power of the whole class, hang posters for children to study until they're ready to go on to the next batch.   JANE HILLARD

Attack Of The Killer B's

Try this playful bulletin-board activity to help students build their vocabularies. Attach a large cutout beehive to the bulletin board. All around the hive, post large cutout bees. On each bee's body, print a word beginning with the letter B. Title the board, "Conquering Killer B's." Have children look up the words on the bees and learn their definitions. Then, after giving students sufficient time to learn all the words, call out a different B word each morning. Pupils should then write the word on a slip of paper, define it, and use it correctly in an original sentence. After the class has mastered the B of the day, place that Killer B in the hive. Continue until all the bees are safely in the beehive.   SANDRA J. FREY

Print Hint

Ever notice that students can recognize sight words on flashcards but not in library books? Here's a game to improve sight-word recognition.

First choose 20 sight words. Look for the words printed in a variety of type styles, colors, and sizes in newspapers and magazines, then cut out several examples of each word. Prepare one game card per student by taping 16 words onto each cardboard card in rows of four by four. Cover cards with clear contact paper.

Now play sight-word bingo by calling out words from the list of 20. Children use dried beans to cover words on their cards. The first to fill a row across, down, or diagonally wins. Kids swap cards and play again.   ANNA COTTON

Vocabulary Building

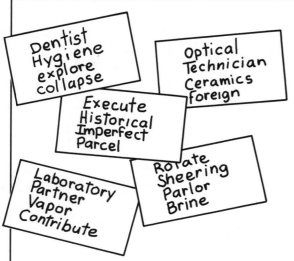

Dentist
Hygiene
explore
collapse

Optical
Technician
Ceramics
foreign

Execute
Historical
Imperfect
Parcel

Laboratory
Partner
Vapor
Contribute

Rotate
Sheering
Parlor
Brine

Vocabulary Practice

Enrich students' vocabulary skills with this team activity. Pair off students, then give each two-person team four index cards each day. Ask each team to write four new words located during their assignments each day. Encourage teammates to quiz each other periodically on their personalized vocabulary list. Kids could also ask their parents or other adults about vocabulary that might be unique to their business or profession. Teams can add these to daily lists too. Then, set aside a special vocabulary time each week. Ask teammates to choose one word from their list to challenge other teams to correctly use the special vocabulary word in a sentence. Allow one point to the team for each word that stumps the class.

SHEILA BERENSON

Bone Up On Words

A Bone Up On Words program promotes word recognition and pronunciation skills. Here's how one reading resource teacher developed it. She first identified and listed a total of 1,738 words from classroom reading materials at each grade level. Next she recruited a team of community volunteers, each committed to spending one hour a week at the school. These grandparents, mothers, fathers and other volunteers were trained via a videotaped practice session to use the word list in one-on-one work with students. Finally, teachers invited parents to sign their children up for the program. In doing so, parents agreed to encourage their children's participation and help them study words at home.

All students, regardless of grade level, begin with level-one words, then move along at their own pace. When a word poses a problem for a student, the volunteer notes the word and returns to it at the end of the session. The student spells and pronounces the word again, and if it's still a problem, the volunteer works with the student in developing a strategy for decoding the word. Volunteers also pick up on words that students can pronounce but do not understand and give tips for remembering the meanings. Troublesome words are listed on a study sheet, which parents have agreed to follow up on at home. These words are addressed first the following week.

Upon passing all the words on a grade-level list, each student is awarded a certificate, color-coded by levels. A color-coded bone with the student's name is also placed on a bulletin board in the main foyer, recognizing this child as an expert at that level.

This portion of the program is supplemented by a daily Bone Up Mystery Word Contest, which provides students with an opportunity to encounter words at all grade levels. Words from the master list are put on color-coded bones. Each color corresponds to a different grade level. The bones are then grouped by grade level and each group is displayed in a different area of the school.

Every morning on the intercom, a student announcer gives clues for one of those words. Clues include number of letters in the word, its various meanings as different parts of speech, and the color or grade level of the word. Students are encouraged to use the clues to identify the mystery word among words displayed in that grade-level's group. The mystery word is announced and defined the following morning, and previous words of that week are reviewed.

There's no doubt about Bone Up On Words' success. Kids not involved in the program are begging for sign-up forms. Volunteers say participating students stop them in the hall to tell them they are studying. And teachers are finding more than improved word pronunciation skills. "It creates a positive feeling for the students," they say, "and lets children see that parents are interested in reading."

Vocabulary Building

Dead Words

Are your students' descriptive vocabularies limited to the words good, nice, cool, awesome and bad? It's difficult for students to write creatively with such limited vocabularies. Here's a possible solution: make a dead word bulletin board. Write each overused word on a tombstone made of grey construction paper complete with the letters R.I.P. (after all, the goal is to let the overused words rest in peace). Brainstorm or use a thesaurus to find words to replace the "dead" words. List the alternative words next to the tombstone. KENNA LOXTERMAN

Won-der-ful Windows

Introduce three-, four-, and five-syllable words using a windowed oaktag device and word strips. Fold in half a 4-by 10-inch piece of oaktag and seal lengthwise. Cut out five windows, spaced 1/2 inch apart. Divide vocabulary word into syllables. Write the syllables, 3/4 inch apart, on a 1-by 12-inch strip of oaktag. As the student pulls the strip, he or she pronounces each syllable as it appears in a window, until the whole word is revealed. Then ask students to use each word in a sentence. SALLY LAUB

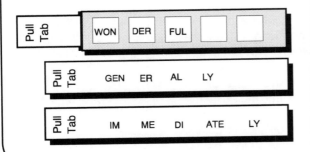

Map It Out!

Large index cards and these six steps help kids learn new words. Students: 1. Draw five 2-inch circles on a card — one in the center and one in each corner. 2. Print the new word in the middle circle. 3. Print the word phonetically in the upper-right circle. 4. Write a brief definition of the word in the lower-right circle. 5. Write a sentence using the word and underline the word in the lower-left circle. 6. Illustrate the word in the upper-left circle. Just the process of making the card boosts memory. MARIA VALERIE-GOLD

Colorful Language

Every first grader learns the eight colors found in a basic crayon box. Expand your students' color awareness by discussing words that bring particular colors to mind. List on the board: embarrassed, sad, pure, gloomy, hot, blushing, death, guilty, winter, angry, spring, loud, Fourth of July, peppermint, evil, money, envious, night, somber, dramatic, fresh, sallow, exciting, good, bad, dingy, autumn, salad, surrender, wild, sunny, healthy. Talk about colors that seem to go with each word and how some words will evoke the same color response from people while others are much more open to interpretation. Ask kids to share other words and colors that go together.

Next, give kids a list of colors that are more unusual and ask them to find examples. The list could include: ebony, scarlet, turquoise, henna, ruby, cerulean, mauve, vermillion, chartreuse, tawny, magenta, salmon, khaki, coral, and ivory.

As children become familiar with the more unusual colors and color-mood words, make class lists using these words in interesting similes and word pictures: Her blush was as scarlet as a wild, autumn sunset.

Your class will enjoy "coloring up" their vocabulary and finding examples of colors in songs, science, literature, and sports.
BEATRICE BACHRACH PERRI

Semantics

Semantic Antics

Increase students' word power and broaden their appreciation of language with these challenging word games.

Portmanteau Words

Portmanteau words are created by blending two words. Lewis Carroll used portmanteau words in his poem "Jabberwocky" — chortle (from chuckle and snort) and galumph (from gallop and triumph).

Print several well-known portmanteaus — motel, brunch, smog — on individual cards. On the back of each card write the two original words and brief definition. To play, divide the class into two teams. To score a point, a team member draws a card, pronounces the word, identifies the two words which were blended to create the new word, and used the portmanteau in a sentence. Ask students to create and define their own portmanteaus based on interests — vidames (video games) or draint (draw and paint).

Malapropisms

Malapropisms are ridiculous misuses of language, involving words that sound similar but have entirely different meanings — typhoon/tycoon, alligator/elevator, abdominal/abominable. Play Malapropism Quiz Bowl with your class. Divide the class into two teams. Prepare cards with printed sentences containing malapropisms. One member from each team comes up to the front of the room. Place a buzzer or bell between the two players. Draw a card and read the sentence aloud. Students try to identify the malapropism and supply the correct word. The first player to hit the bell or to clap hands gets the first chance to answer. If incorrect, the other player has a try. Score one point for each correct answer.

Oxymorons

Oxymorons are phrases which use two contradictory words to provide emphasis — cruel kindness, sweet sorrow, war games. Print individual words on separate cards. Kids play Oxymoron Concentration, turning over two cards at a time, saying the words together as a phrase, and deciding if it is an oxymoron. Ask children to create their own oxymorons and to explain their choice of words.

Neologisms

Neologisms are new words or phrases that have become an accepted part of everyday vocabulary — clone, digital, software.

To create a deck of neologisms to use in a game of Neology Bluff, ask students to ask parents and other adults for new words. As each locates a neologism, he or she prints the word on a card. On the back, the student writes the definition in red and two false, but logical, definitions in black.

When you have a stack of neologisms, divide the class into two teams. Three players from one team stand in front of the room. One player shows the word to the opposing team, pronounces it, and gives one of the definitions on the back of the card. The second player gives another definition and the third player provides the last definition. The opposing team must identify the correct definition in order to score. Alternate turns.

KELLY RILEY

Fact Or Fiction

Try this game, based on the old TV game show To Tell the Truth, to reinforce vocabulary words. Place five dictionaries at a table, then choose a panel of five students. Place your word list on the board where the entire class can see it. Panelists first secretly choose the one who will "tell the truth" — by giving the actual definition of the first word. The other four panelists must fake their definitions. After the panelists recite their definitions, the students in the "audience" write down the name of the panelist whom they think told the truth. Then the panelist who did recite the correct definition stands up. The panelist who fools the most students gets one point. Audience members who identify the real definition get two points. Change panelists every few words.

LINDA BOND BYRD

Comprehension

Comprehending Pro's

Help kids strengthen reading comprehension skills — stating main ideas, finding details, recalling information — by playing Compro during group time. To play, select one passage from a student text for children to read silently. When everyone finishes, kids close their books and write as many details from the passage as they can recall. Then each player takes a turn reading aloud his or her list. If other students have the same details on their lists, all students, including the reader, must cross off those details. After each has had a turn, players receive one point for each detail not recalled by others.

LINDA ROTT

Piece It Together

Clip short, one-column newspaper articles in half vertically. Give the left halves to students. They tape them to a piece of paper, allowing room for writing on the right side of the paper.

Students determine the main idea of the story from remaining words and fill in words to complete the article. Remaining word parts and letters from the cut version must be used.

Students then discuss their interpretations of their articles. Allow them to see the second half of the article after they have completed their own version.

SANDRA FREY

What Will Happen Next?

Predicting and Decision Making

Help develop prediction, comprehension, and decision-making skills with this group reading activity.

First, choose a story for group reading and have children read the title of the story only. Using the information from the title, ask kids to make guesses as to what they think the story is about. Next, have kids read silently at their own rate, stopping them at several predetermined points (for example, the second paragraph on page 10). When everyone has reached that point, ask students what they think the characters will do next (divergent thinking) or what they can't do at this point (convergent thinking). To improve concentration, ask kids to find plot clues as they are reading; afterwards, ask questions relating to the plot clues, such as "When did you first suspect that..." or "When did you begin to get the idea that the character would..."

After they've finished the story, have kids evaluate what they have just read, including behavior of the characters, setting, or plot.

KATHY FAGGELLA

Under The Umbrella

To help children grasp the concept of the main idea in a short piece of writing, try this exercise. Copy a simple paragraph onto the chalkboard, then sketch an outline of an umbrella underneath it. Have children find the sentence that contains the main idea of the paragraph, then write it inside the umbrella; all other sentences should go under the umbrella. Children should pick and choose sentences until they find the correct one. The process helps children visualize the concept — and they seem to enjoy it too!

JACQUELINE POMPHRET

Kiddie Cliffhangers

Children will love writing an ending to your storytime book! Have the students write the ending after you have read one or two chapters aloud. Read a few of the students' conclusions to the class. Then continue reading the story. Did anyone predict the outcome of the story or write a better one?

JUDY VAN ACKER

Comprehension

Shopping For Facts And Opinions

Here's a fun way to teach students to distinguish between fact and opinion.

Cut two long rectangular strips of cardboard to serve as game boards. Label one "Fact Shop" and the other "Opinion Shop." Draw shelves on each strip of paper to look like a real store.

Print names of familiar products and a fact or opinion about the products on pieces of paper cut to fit the spaces on the "shelves." Shuffle the pieces of paper and place them facedown on a table. A student chooses a piece of paper, reads it and places it in a shelf in the proper "shop."

This game can be played with a group or one student.   ANNE PACHECO

Sentence Sequencing

Divide the class into teams of three or four pupils each. Give each team an identical copy of a paragraph in which the order of the sentences has been completely mixed up. In addition, give each team a piece of paper, scissors and paste. The object of this activity is for the students to cut and paste the sentences into proper sequence. Each group must be able to explain why the topic sentence and supporting sentences are presented in the order in which they have placed them. Some variations in sentence order may be accepted, as long as each group has a good reason for its decisions. BARBARA LASSMAN

Story Sequence

When your class has finished reading a story or novel, try this game for practice in sequencing events. Pick 10 major events in the story. Write a sentence that describes each event. Print the first half of each sentence on one sheet of paper, in the order in which the events occurred. Print the ending of each sentence on a separate slip of paper. Place in a learning center. Students pair sentence beginnings with the endings.
MARY BURMAN

Read All About It

Try this newspaper scavenger hunt to encourage reading and critical-thinking skills.

Divide students into groups of four or five. Hand out construction paper, glue, scissors, and one or two editions of your local newspaper. Tell students that within a specified time, they must find, glue down, and label the following items:
- A newspaper masthead
- An index
- A classified ad
- Two letters to the editor; one angry, one complimentary
- A story about, or reference to, children
- A story about a city within 100 miles of your hometown
- The temperature of a city in a southern state
- A sports headline with an accompanying photo

Display children's finished products on the bulletin board.   PAULA HAMILTON

Comprehension

Reading Tapes

Parents who want to help their children with reading-comprehension questions often aren't sure how. To help, tape-record your reading groups throughout the week. Children then check out the tapes for home use. This way, parents can pick up hints on how to ask those very important inferential comprehension questions.
GAIL KOSTKA

Color Reading

Develop students' reading comprehension skills by having them read "in color." To begin, select interesting articles from the local newspaper or from a weekly magazine and make a copy of one article for each child. Ask each to use three different light-colored markers to highlight comprehension information — one color to highlight the main idea, a second to highlight two main points, and a third to highlight three details. When students finish, ask them to give reasons for choosing the information they colored. After some practice, you might ask children to color additional information, such as time/event chronology, topic sentences, and cause/effect relationships.
MANNY MARTIN

Read, Team, Read

Try this team-game approach to perk up vocabulary and reading comprehension practice.

Write vocabulary words on the chalkboard or an overhead projector. Divide the reading group into two teams. Select a word for a member of Team One. The student has 10 seconds to pronounce the word and give its meaning. If this student is unable to answer correctly, the first player from Team Two gets a chance.

Set a scoring goal for the activity. For example, a list of 15 words represents a total score of 30 points. An appropriate goal would be a minimum score of 24.

Adapt this procedure for comprehension practice. Create questions on following directions, using pages from next week's workbook assignments. Players skim directions to identify the type of response required — write a letter, circle a word, write a paragraph.

Practice reading skills such as locating main idea and using context clues. Students from Team One read short paragraphs as players from Team Two ask questions about the paragraph. Award points for "stumpers" as well as each correct answer.
JIM HAWES

Recipes For Reading

Interested in a tasteful way to build vocabulary and comprehension skills? All you need is a variety of cake-mix boxes, cereal cartons, and labels from frozen foods. Make up questions about specific cooking directions and nutritional information given on the packages. For example: What must you do to the cake pan before you pour batter into it? or Which contains more vitamin A — pudding or gelatin? Write questions on cards and note the answers on the back, laminate, then mount packaging and cards on a decorated bulletin board. Ask children to bring in labels and boxes to make up questions to stump their classmates.
PATRICIA WARREN

Reading Motivators

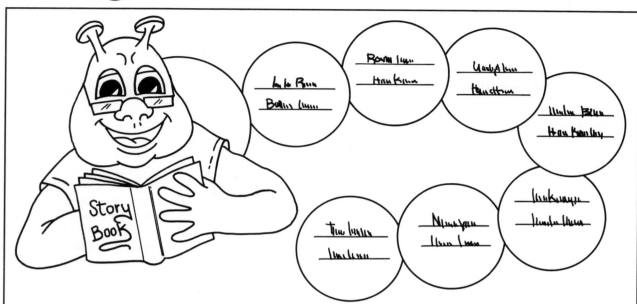

Recipe For Reading Success

If you have difficulty encouraging your students to read, try the following idea. Make a cut-paper bookworm. The object is to make the worm grow by adding segments until it reaches a predetermined destination. Design a colorful worm head and attach it to the top of a bulletin board in your classroom. Tell students to read to parents and sisters, brothers, aunts, uncles, grandparents or neighbors.

Since first-grade-level books are short, have students write the book titles in composition books and have listeners initial them. Periodically, children should bring the composition books to school and receive duplicated worm segments on which the book titles and their names are written. Then cut out the segments and attach to the worm to form its body. Staple the segments to string to make it easier to stretch across walls or ceilings.

For older children, segments could be given for reading time spent or number of pages read. These students place their book titles and names on the segments themselves. As the worm grows, interest increases. GAIL J. HARTSOUGH

Bread Bag Bookmark

Encourage reading with colorful, sturdy bookmarks, which students can make by themselves. Ask kids to collect the plastic clips used to reseal bread bags — each child will need at least five. To make the bookmark, each student measures and cuts a 7-inch strip of inch-wide fabric. The student threads one end of the strip through the hole in a clip, and pastes it to the flat part of the clip. The child slips a second clip onto the strip, pasting it just below the bottom of the first clip. Continue until five bread clips are pasted to the fabric. Leave an end dangling below the last clip.
JANE PRIEWE

Reading Motivators

Heard It Through The Intercom

Make your school intercom a part of your reading program. Try these ways to turn it into a powerful teaching tool!

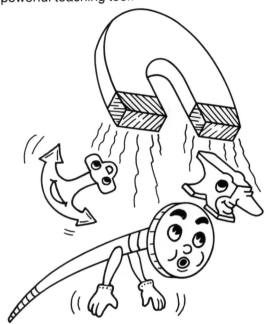

What Word Am I?: This variation of a "word-of-the-week" program will have kids thinking analytically every day. First determine a "word-of-the-week." Supply one clue to the word each day, Monday through Thursday. For example, for the word magnet, clues might include: has two poles; was named after Magnesia, Greece; valuable as a direction finder; has the power to attract other substances.

By class or individually, have students use the clues to identify the word, then place their answers in a designated box. The presenter announces the word and the winners on Friday.

Tell Me More: Choose a high-interest book to read over the intercom and divide it into parts to be read each day. Try to end each session with a cliff-hanger.

JUMANJI, by Chris Van Allsburg (Houghton Mifflin, 1981) is a great book to begin with. It takes about three days to read, at 5 to 10 minutes a session, and can be enjoyed by the entire school.

Weather Report: Choose a different student each day or week to broadcast a weather forecast over the intercom. Based on which grades the

forecast will be broadcast to, determine a list of items to be covered, such as high and low temperatures, wind speed, barometric pressure, or predictions for weather conditions at recess, after school, or the following day.

Have student reporters gather current information from newspapers and other available sources and write cue cards for each presentation. Classes tuned in to the forecast can chart or map weather conditions as reported and use this information to make additional predictions.

Trivia Trail: When you use the intercom for this version of trivia, the whole school will have fun getting to know reference materials.

First identify particular categories, for example, places, minerals, authors, animals, or famous firsts. Have each student do some research on an item within one of the categories and write four clues about his or her choice. For example, a student who chooses "Minnesota," within the category "places," might come up with the following clues: This state has more than 10,000 lakes. It has the largest open-pit iron mine in the world. It is the 12th largest state in America. The state bird is the common loon.

Each week, a different student presenter announces the category and one clue on Monday, followed by another clue each day through Thursday. Encourage students to make use of available reference materials, including textbooks, almanacs, atlases, and dictionaries to research the clues and identify the person, place, or thing.

You might want to present two sets of trivia to involve different levels of students. Announce the correct answer on Friday and encourage students to share how they used the clues and reference materials to track down their answers.

Reading Motivators

Celebrate Reading Week

Set aside a week as Celebrate Reading Week. Try these ideas:

You're on the air! Ask students to share their enthusiasm for reading with others by broadcasting a five-minute morning book talk on the PA system. Volunteers can discuss highlights of recently read books. Or, invite guests — such as the principal, custodian, librarian — to share books from their childhoods.

Read-along and along. Write the first sentence of a story on a strip of paper. For example: The other day at recess I saw a baby dinosaur on the playground. Hang the sentence outside your door. Ask students to take turns adding a sentence strip to continue the story. As the story stretches along the hallway, ask the class next door to take over. Invite visiting parents and school staff to contribute, too. Encourage students to tack up illustrations of story scenes around the strips.

Share a story. Ask your librarian to make a list of good read-aloud stories. Then invite fellow staffers, school board members, and the superintendent to read to your class at a time that's mutually convenient. Advise them that the librarian can suggest books your kids would enjoy. Place a student in charge of sending a thank-you note to each reader.

Treasure Hunt. Follow the procedure for a standard treasure hunt: Provide one clue at a time for student teams to work on together. Each clue leads to a place where a letter of the alphabet

— and the next clue — are waiting. When all are collected, the letters spell out the location of the treasure.

For a more reading-oriented treasure hunt, relate the clues to events or characters in popular children's books. The correct answer should signal where the next clue can be found.

A celebration sampler. What do students think is the best way to celebrate reading? Read a favorite book with a younger child? Design a perfect reading nook? Hand out 4-inch squares of paper and ask each child to make a drawing of or to describe a perfect salute. Glue squares together on a colorful background and display.

Reading lists. How many different kinds of items do you read in a week? Maps? Menus? Magazines? What else? Ask kids to come up with a list that ranges from the most common materials to the most unusual.

Celebration box. Every classroom has potential creators of original games, plays, recipes, and stories. Solicit contributions from your students, then ask for creative work from other students and teachers in school. Organize all original materials in a reading resource box in the library for everyone in the school to enjoy.

Grand finale. Gather fun-loving colleagues and do a presentation for your kids. Perform excerpts from favorite children's books or do individual readings as book characters. It'll be a performance all will remember! NANCY BATES

Reading Motivators

Adopt-A-Book

When I realized that some of the best books in our school library were not leaving the shelves, I became concerned. I soon discovered the reason. The covers on these books were worn and tattered, and the kids probably thought these volumes would be dull and uninteresting.

I then came up with an idea: a book-adoption program. I explained to my students that these tattered books were lonely and needed a lot of love. I then told the kids that they were all eligible to "adopt" one of these lonely books. To qualify, each child must read one book of his or her choice, write a short review, and design an original book jacket for it. We later laminated the book jackets and re-covered the books with them. Students were soon clamoring to read the adopted books!

To wrap up the project, I conducted a class discussion on the criteria each of us uses when selecting a book. We then discussed ways in which we could improve our selection methods in the future.   DOROTHY BOWERS

Comic Corner

Make a comic corner where your students line up to leave the classroom. Mount cartoons and comics clipped from the newspaper on construction paper. Laminate the comics for durability and display.

Keep a file of the comics and cartoons used. Color code the comics for vocabulary words, social studies, science, language arts, idioms and expressions, etc. Label the back of the comic with each specific word or subject. There are many comics about holidays, feelings, report cards, book reports, music lessons, etc.

You'll notice that even the slower readers are anxious to read what is posted in the Comic Corner each week.   LUANN WILLIAMS

Rebasal Reading

Dust off old basal readers and story anthologies from the bookroom and include them as choices for voluntary reading. Lead kids to discover these old books with a sign saying: "This is what they read in the 'old days'!" Suggest that anyone finding a particularly good story point it out to other students by way of a homemade bookmark. Ask each child who reads a story because of a bookmark to sign the bookmark.

                    MARGARET HOAGLAND

Read Everything From A To Z

Show the many things we read in daily life with this display. Make a caption from construction paper that reads "Read everything from A to Z." Display one item that begins with each letter of the alphabet. Label items with colored paper.

                    LAURA DAVIS

Recycling Commercial Catalogs

Use commercial catalogs in the classroom to expand thinking and reading skills. Remove the order blanks from several catalogs and have the students fill out orders, figuring the total cost of merchandise, tax and shipping.

Ask students to determine what time the company is open for business. If no toll-free number is given, ask students, what time would it be least expensive to call?

Have students position their companies on a U.S. map.

Make a large chart comparing what goods the catalogs offer, how items are illustrated, who would use the catalog, and prices and methods of payment. CAROL SMALLWOOD

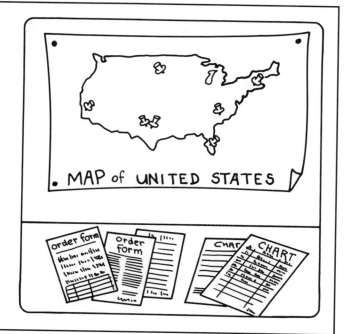

Rookie Readers

Motivate your students to read with this board. Make a baseball player or baseball equipment from construction paper and place in the middle of the board. Cut baseballs from white construction paper. Add stitching with black marker. Write students' names on the baseballs. For every book a student reads, he or she earns a star on his or her baseball.
LU ALICE KAMPWERTH

Beach Bums

To encourage thoughts of summer reading, try this beach-inspired reading center.

In a corner of your classroom, set up items needed for a day at the beach — lounge chairs, beach umbrellas, a rubber raft, an inflatable wading pool, pails and shovels, a beach towel, etc. After students have completed regular work, issue "beach passes" for 10 to 15 minutes of quiet reading on the "beach."

Reading Clues

A bulletin board will encourage kids to ask, "Who's reading that?" Ask school staff to contribute samples of reading material that they think is characteristic of their interests. Choose four to display, without identifying the contributors. Samples might include a horoscope clipping, a recipe card, a travel brochure, a classified ad, an owner's manual for a car, or a book jacket. Ask students to study the display and to guess the identity of each mystery reader. Each child writes the staff names on a slip of paper and tacks it to the board. At the end of the week, announce the winners and ask these students to help arrange the next display. SARA THROOP

Reading Motivators

Reading Circus

Promote reading with this colorful display. Make various circus acts using construction paper and yarn (for the trapeze). Ask each child to draw a clown with chubby arms and legs to allow ample space for decorating. Students brightly color the clowns and write their names on the clowns' suits. Each student must read five books to receive a colored gummed circle. They stick the circles on the clowns' suits. The more disks the students earn, the brighter the clowns look.

MARTHA ESHELMAN

Books Sandwiched In

A lunchtime program on reading helps pupils discover a whole new world of books. Read about one school's program.

Presentations often include hands-on audience participation. This year, kids have applied clown makeup with a visiting clown, performed skits with the high school theater group, learned about pets with an in-house puppy, and shared their own stories with local authors. And there's always time for questions and discussion.

Enthusiasm for Books Sandwiched In is contagious, and teachers find that the program's success spills over into the classroom. Pupils come back to the classroom talking authors and titles, and books become social conversations instead of academic ones. It puts books and the library in a more intimate, fun light, and that, teachers say, has some kids signing up a year in advance for Books Sandwiched In sessions.

Idea Lists

Need ideas to keep reading spirit high? Send a list around your building and ask teachers to share three successful techniques. Or circulate a list in your district.

Here are a few to get you started: Create a book museum, with kids designing exhibits on favorite books and displaying "artifacts" from the story. Kids might also write a sequel to a favorite book; hold a trial to defend an opinion of a book with class members as the jury; create a dance that tells the story; ask a local newspaper if it would publish a children's book review column.

Don't forget to ask students which projects they have done that helped them understand and appreciate books the most. Add their favorites to the list, then share it with colleagues.

KATHERINE FISHER   MARY ANNE LECOS

Reading Aloud

Read-Aloud Activities

You've finished reading a story to your class — now what? Here's a list of suggestions to enhance, extend, and enliven the ideas in the story.

As a group, make up a short rhyme which tells about the story you've read. Write the poem on the chalkboard and ask kids to copy it as handwriting practice.

Make a poster with the title and author of the book and ask kids to autograph it with their comments. After volunteers decorate the poster, hang it on the wall outside your classroom.

Encourage students to make up a new character for the story. Kids can add this character to some adventure or interaction with the other story characters and can write their ideas individually or as a group.

Write the names of the characters on the board. Volunteers take the roles of characters and act out scenes.

Ask groups of kids to write a letter to one of the characters in the story, telling him or her what they would have done if they had been in the same situation.
VICKI FOOTE

Laughing and Learning

Look toward literature as a source of humorous incidents your kids can chuckle over together. By reading a funny story aloud, sharing the fun, and extending those good feelings to related activities, you'll help students develop their individual wit as well as group spirit. Here are several books that are good for a chuckle. I CAN DO IT ALL BY MYSELF by Shigeo Watanabe (Putnam series, 1985), ages 5-7. The delightful misadventures of a little bear lend themselves to humorous, satisfying experiences for young children. Share one book in the series, HOW DO I PUT IT ON? Then gather two sets of oversized clothes. Place each set in a shopping bag. Divide children into two teams and give each team a bag of clothes. In relay form, kids take turns putting the clothes on (buttons buttoned, zippers zipped) and taking them off. Everyone can share a laugh at the comic antics.

At about age 7, slapstick humor is tops. Kids can find plenty in HOMER PRICE by Robert McCloskey (Houghton Mifflin, 1981), ages 7-10. In the book, Homer's uncle invents a machine to simplify making donuts. Homer tries to operate it and bedlam begins. If you're feeling brave, try reinventing, or at least replicating, the process of donut-making. Assign duties to measurers, mixers, rollers, and shapers. Do the frying yourself. Everyone can be a taster. Then compare your experience to Homer's. You might even write a story together about your experience, including funny observations and descriptions.

Dr. Seuss books provide zany characters whose unexpected antics, imaginative shapes, and creative names can inspire children to play with language. Share McELLIGOT'S POOL (E.M. Hale, 1947), all ages. In the story, a young man fishes in a small puddle and catches quite a surprise. Post a large paper pond and invite children to create their own inventive fish to fill it up. Ask kids to give their creatures names the way Dr. Seuss did. Add a few of your own.

In NOTHING EVER HAPPENS ON MY BLOCK by Ellen Raskin (Atheneum, 1966), Chester Filbert remains oblivious to the most exciting things. Read the book together and then take a walk. When you return, review your walk and take turns verbally transforming what you did see into something wild and fun.
DEE HOPKINS   MARGARET B. NARDI

Biography

Book Party

Culminate a unit on biographies with a class party at which the guests of honor are the subjects of the books.

Make sure each pupil has chosen a different person to read about. After they've finished reading their books, distribute a question sheet and ask students to answer the questions in the first person, as if they were the subjects of the biographies. Possible questions include:
• When and where were you born?
For what are you famous?
• For what would you like to be remembered?
• Which person or persons do you admire and why?
• Tell about an amusing (or tragic or frightening) event that happened in your past.
• Did you ever marry? If so, do you have children?

On party day, give each student a name tag with his or her character's name on it, and explain that for the next hour or so they are to assume the identities of the people they've read about. During the party, encourage students to mingle and share facts from their answer sheets. Each student should find out as much as possible about at least one other person in the room.

SUSAN K. BYRNES

Biography Binge

Who's Emily Dickinson? What's so important about George Washington Carver? Did anyone ever write a book about Bruce Springsteen? Your students will answer these questions and more when you organize a biography binge.

Set aside a few weeks to focus on biography as a genre. Give kids time to browse through the biography section of your school or public library. Ask them to think about what they would hope to learn when reading a person's life story. Then, together, construct a biography report form. Brainstorm ways to share information with one another. For example, set aside time each day for a few kids to contribute to Facts About the Famous.

Encourage students who are interested in one person to read on. Biographies by other writers can add perspective.

ETHEL T. GRIFFIN

The Name Game

Try this game when reviewing information about story characters, famous people from history, or current newsmakers. Write the names of people students are reviewing on separate slips of paper, and allow one for each child. Choose one student to start the game. Without letting him or her see the name, tape a slip of paper on the student's back. The child shows the name to classmates, then tries to figure out the famous person's identity by asking questions of the class. Kids may ask only questions that can be answered with yes or no. For example, "Do I play sports?" or "Am I the leader of a country?" When the student discovers his or her secret identity, or has asked 10 questions, remove the name tag and choose a new player.

GERTRUDE PARKER

Poetry, Around the World

Literature From Around the World

Display a large world map in the classroom. As students read books about different places around the world or by authors from foreign countries, have them place cards on the corresponding locations on the map. Use a small picture or illustration to represent the title, author, illustrator, or characters. As the year progresses and you begin to notice bare spots on the map, ask the school or town librarian to help you find book selections that represent this missing country or ethnic group.

A Pocketful Of Poems

My first-grade class reads a great deal of poetry. One of the first poems we read, "Put a Poem in Your Pocket" by Beatrice Schenk deRegniers, quickly became a class favorite. In response to kids' enthusiasm, I created a poetry bulletin board to highlight and categorize other favorite poems. Here's how: First, hang a colorful shoe bag on the bulletin board with enough pockets to hold several poems; label the pockets according to seasons or themes your class is studying. After kids read additional poems, place them in the pockets of the shoe bag for easy access. As the seasons or themes change, so do the poems.

CHERYL M. HAAKE

Reading Around the World

Make reading more of an adventure this year with a home-based, all-school or classroom project that has international flair.

All teachers in your school may like to participate in a "Reading Around the World" program, perhaps with the reading coordinator as project supervisor. Decide on 10 countries to focus on — one per school month — and hang large outline drawings of the countries around the school. Each class gets a paper airplane with the teacher's name written on it, and all classes start on the same country. At the end of each month, a class's airplane flies to another country if 75 percent of the group has met the nightly reading requirement — reading independently at home for 15 minutes on five days, or on five days having an adult read to the child or listen to the child read.

Children track their reading activity with a home reading passport. The passport can be a small notebook of lined paper with a dark blue paper cover. If your funds allow, have a stamp made up with your own reading program seal for marking each passport cover. Each evening, the child or parent notes in the passport what was read, who read it, and for how long.

To make this a classroom program, give each child a paper airplane. Individuals fly to a different country each month if they have completed home reading requirements. Give children a reward to note each "flight"—such as an outline badge of the new country or a paper bookmark of the country's flag (laminate for durability).

Introduce each month's country by reading aloud to the class from a book about it or by cooking a dish together that's representative of the country's cuisine. Encourage children to learn all they can about the country they're "visiting." FAMILIES THE WORLD OVER is a good children's book series about life in foreign lands. Included in the set are books focusing on China, Egypt, France, India, Jamaica, Nigeria, Pakistan, Sri Lanka, and West Germany. (Write Lerner Publications, 241 First Ave., N., Minneapolis, MN 55401.)

SUSAN SCHERLING

Sharing Books, Authors, and Illustrators

Illustrating As An Illustrator

Students can be taught to notice and use specific illustrator styles. For example, Leo Lionni has a distinct style that children love to use. One of Lionni's storybook characters is a mouse made of torn construction paper. Students can make their own tear-art creatures.

They can browse through books and use an illustrator's style to illustrate their own books or invent their own style.

STACY M. ROSS

Author Display

Brainstorm with your students about ways in which they might share their favorite authors with other students in the classroom. Suggest they work in groups to collect all the books by a particular author, such as Clyde Robert Bulla or Ruth Chew. Then have kids make annotated, illustrated bibliographies of these books for other students, classes, or the school or town library. In addition, have kids make a bulletin board or hallway display, give oral book reports, or read aloud from author's works.

Reading Bubbles

Here's a way to get students thinking about characters in a story. Show kids a comic strip with the characters' dialogue and thoughts in bubbles. Then ask each child to draw a large bubble for the main character of a story the class has just read and to fill the bubble with traits or behavior of that character. Suggest that kids make specific references to the story, such as "helped his mom do the dishes" or "she practiced for the big game." When kids finish, draw a huge bubble on a large piece of poster board and list all the traits kids included in their individual bubbles. Beneath the bubble, draw a picture of the character or use an opaque projector to trace an illustration in the book.   ROSE REISSMAN

Book Buddies

Selecting a book for someone else is an art. Here's an activity to help students develop that expertise.

Pair up kids and ask partners to ask questions of each other. Explain that the aim is to get to know the partner well enough to select a book for him or her. Before partners begin, develop as a class a list of sample questions: Do you like fiction or nonfiction? What are your hobbies? Remind students to take notes during the interview.

When all partners have been interviewed, give kids time to search for books for their buddies. Then ask kids to exchange books and read for 15 minutes. If a student doesn't like the selection, he or she may choose another. Discuss how successful kids were at selecting books that their peers enjoyed.

PHYLLIS GOOTEE   MARGARET MAHLER

Who Done It

Make a large fingerprint to decorate this bulletin board. Next, post clues to the identity of well-known book characters or historical figures. At the end of the week, fill in the "wanted" personalities. Give kids a chance to make up clues, too.

SUE KREIBICH

CLUES
1. First President
2. Would not tell a lie.
3. chopped down a cherry tree.
...der of
5. Signed declaration

Teaching Literature to Intermediate Children

Helping children understand and enjoy literature can be tricky. Make literature fun by using some of the following ideas for presenting a literary work to your class:

• Scan the work or selection with the class and identify the words whose meanings they don't know. Using reference materials, work with the class to find the meanings. Then create a glossary of these words.

• Using the glossary, rewrite the work or selection in colloquial language.

• Use the glossary to add footnotes to pages.

• Dramatize poems or a chapter impromptu or with a script.

• Create a collage to illustrate the work.

• Create a comic strip about the work.

• Chart the life of a character.

• Write the biography of a character from the work.

• Have students create puppets and give a puppet show following the plot of the work.

• Create a bulletin board depicting the life of an author or display his or her works.

• Teach the art of storytelling including pitch, loudness, rates, pauses and gestures. Then have students "tell" one of their favorite works to the class. LINDA HOLLINGSWORTH-BROWN

Scientific Fiction

Have fun with science and literature by introducing students to Robert McClung's science books on animals and insects, including MAJOR: THE STORY OF A BLACK BEAR (Linnet Books, 1988). Combine these books with your science curriculum and ask students to research animals that interest them in order to write and illustrate their own science mini-books. Encourage kids to read their books to younger students.

Fun With Rebus Books

Allow students to discover the fun of rebus books by sharing THE LITTLE RED RIDING HOOD REBUS BOOK by Ann Morris, illustrated by Ljiljana Rylands (Orchard Books, 1987). Students can then work individually or in small groups to write their own rebus version of a classic fairy or folktale such as Cinderella, Paul Bunyan, The Three Little Pigs, and so on. Help kids make ink-print stamps to represent repeated words found in the story or use the computer to print out picture symbols. Children will also enjoy creating their own Rebus dictionary to accompany their stories.
LYNN MINDERMAN

Celebrate Children's Book Illustrators

Wordless picture books are an excellent way to get kids excited about reading. Begin by having students look through wordless books, such as NEW BABY & SCHOOL (Harper and Row, 1987) by Emily Arnold McCully or JUMANJI by Chris Van Allsburg (Houghton Mifflin, 1981). Divide the class into groups of two or three students each to write narratives to accompany the pictures in the books. Later, children can give dramatic readings of their chosen stories, each taking the part of a specific character. As a follow-up activity, have students create their own wordless picture books to share with classmates.

Sharing Books, Authors, and Illustrators

Book Recommendation Display

Have students create an interests/hobbies bulletin board display so that books matching their interests can be recommended throughout the year by you, other students, the librarian, or other teachers. Give students individual spaces on the board to list their names, personal interests (astronomy, snakes, jokes, soccer, gymnastics, drawing, dance), and the types of stories they enjoy (mysteries, adventures, sports stories). Make sure you leave room for recommendations.

Literary Posters

Ask students to create posters that represent their favorite books. If a student chooses TREASURE ISLAND, for example, he or she might draw a picture of Long John Silver, a pirate ship, or a treasure map. Or, the poster could feature descriptive words, such as humble, terrific, radiant for CHARLOTTE'S WEB. Finally, hold a literary poster contest in which students try to guess book titles from each other's posters.
LYNN MINDERMAN

RRRRRead It!

Children are encouraged to recommend books to their fellow students with this springy bulletin board featuring a big green frog relaxing under a mushroom. The frog and mushroom are made of colored butcher paper. Put spots on mushroom in contrasting, light colors. Students write the titles and authors of the books they recommend on these spots.
KAREN STONG

Thematic Reading Boxes

Ask students to create reading boxes for books with themes, such as scary, sad, silly, funny, thrilling, and so on. Paint sturdy cardboard boxes and decorate them with the theme words. Let students stock the boxes with books they find appropriate; allow other students to select books from these boxes for independent reading. Students can bring books to share from home or borrow books from the town or school library. Have kids think of ideas for monthly themes, such as Scary Halloween Tales, Winter Wonderland, or Spring Fever.

Reading Sweepstakes

How to encourage kids to sample a broad range of books? Hold a reading sweepstakes. Give each child a sweepstakes entry folder. Include a sweepstakes record form (see reproducible on p. 26). Also tuck in contest rules and project suggestions. Explain to kids that to be eligible for the sweepstakes drawing, they must read a book from each category box on their form and in some way — oral report, character puppet, diorama, and so forth—share it with the class. Suggested categories: adventure, classic, fairy tale, humor, animal, family mystery, historical, science fiction, play, the arts, sports, biography, poetry, myth, science, travel, and free choice.

Set a specific amount of time to complete all the categories. If you have less time available, create a form with fewer categories. Allow time in class for students to share books with each other. When kids finish, place eligible entries in a hat and draw winners. The prizes? Books, of course.
PAT McMILLION

Reading Sweepstakes Entry

Category	Book Title	Author
Adventure		
Animal		
Classic		
Fairy Tale		
Humor		
Family		
Mystery		
Historical		
Science Fiction		
Play		
Sports		
Biography		
Poetry		
Travel		
Science		

Tree Of Knowledge

Fostering a desire in children to read can be accomplished by making a tree of knowledge.

At the beginning of the year, tape a construction paper tree to a wall.

After the children have successfully finished reading and summarizing a book, they write the title, author and the student's name on a leaf for the tree.

They also write a book file card using a 5x8 index card. On this card they write who, what, where, why and how question about the book to motivate other class members to read it. The child writes the title, author, and states whether the book is fiction or nonfiction at the top of the card. If nonfiction, the child includes the subject matter. It is important not to include answers to the questions on the cards in order to entice other students to read the book.

The cards are arranged into fiction and nonfiction sections of the file box. Nonfiction books are further classified by subject. The students are assigned this librarian job.

During the year, the children watch the growth of the tree, the card file, and their new knowledge which they share with their classmates.

VITA MONASTERO

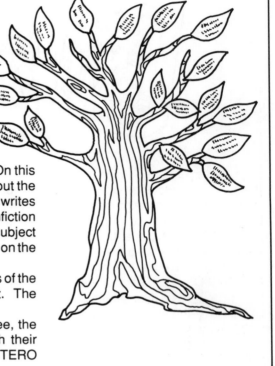

Book Quilt

This fun winter project combines reading and art. Distribute squares of white or pastel paper, and have each pupil draw and color a character or scene from his or her favorite book on the square. The title of the book and the student's name should also be included.

Put a square with the name of your grade or school in the middle of a large sheet of bulletin board paper. Glue the pupils' squares around it, balancing the color and design. If there are empty spaces, fill them in with blank pastel squares. To finish the "quilt," glue a strip of colorful paper to each border and cut a scalloped edge around it for a rippled effect. Add a special touch by gluing small yarn bows to the quilt. The finished creation will motivate readers to explore books that are favorites of their classmates, but new to them.

KATHY BOWLES

Sharing Books, Authors, and Illustrators___

Book Boxes

Book reports become food for thought when properly packaged. This attractive presentation begins with an empty cereal box.

First, run masking tape along the top and bottom of the box to seal all openings. Next, use a knife to cut the box down the middle of the right hand side from top to bottom, so that the box opens like a book. Then cover the exterior and interior of the book-box with paper.

Now each student designs a cover that includes the title and author of the book read. Next, each creates a scene on paper from the selected book and glues it to the interior of the book-box. Then the student uses construction paper to make a pop-up illustration of a main character and glues it to the scene. Finally, the child glues a short book report to the character, to pop out with it.

PATRICIA HESTER

Book Report Blues

To help students understand how to do a book report, try this class project. Read a book to the class, a chapter a day until the entire book is completed. Then ask all your students to use that book for their reports. You can then guide them in answering questions about the plot of the book, the setting, and the important character in the book report format of your choice. ISOBEL L. LIVINGSTONE

What's The Scoop?

Here's a delicious way to have students write book reports. Students use ice cream "scoops" to organize their reports. The top scoop names the book's characters, the middle scoop contains the student's favorite part of the book, and the bottom scoop contains the summary. Students write the title and author of the book on the cone. Top it off with a cherry for fun! Materials needed are colored paper for the scoops, a piece of triangular brown construction paper for the cone, black markers and glue. BONNIE O'MALLEY

2 Writing, Listening, and Speaking

Introduction

Being able to write, listen and speak well are skills everyone needs in order to become successful adults. Yet these skills are often difficult to learn and use effectively. The variety of ideas in this chapter will be invaluable as you help pupils cope with spelling, grammar, handwriting, letter writing, report making, following directions, and listening.

Reinforcing Alphabetical Order

Supply a newspaper section for each pupil. Tell pupils to cut letters from headlines and advertisements and paste them randomly on a piece of plain paper. Then, using a crayon as a "car" or "airplane," have them "drive" their crayon from letter to letter in alphabetical order. Use this same idea with numbers, connecting them in numerical order.
NAOMI E. SMITH

"Alphabits"

To reinforce alphabetical order, cut the large brand names from a variety of cereal boxes and laminate them. Children can help by bringing in cereal boxes from home. Make several sets for children to arrange in alphabetical order. Soon they will not only enjoy working with the colorful words, but will be able to read them, too.
JUDY KEEPORTS

Easy As ABC

To help children with classification skills, try this hands-on alphabetizing activity.

Gather several books from your classroom or school library and ask kids to put them in alphabetical order by title or author's last name. This method is especially helpful for kids who need to physically manipulate objects to gain proficiency in a skill.
KATHY FAGGELLA

Parts of Speech

Rappin' With Language

Have students learn the parts of speech with this rap:

A noun is a person, thing or place: like man or school or the nose on your face.

A pronoun is a sub for nouns: like I and we, you and me, she, her, it, them, they, him, he.

An adjective describes those two: which one? what kind? how many? whose?

A verb is a busy kind of thing: run, walk, must be, try and sing.

An adverb provides lots of info, like how? when? where? yes and no.

Prepositions pull nouns into a phrase: in, on, with, of, and around, are some ways.

Conjunctions connect anything they want: like and, or, nor, so, yet, for, but.

Interjections we use more than we know: wow, ouch, gee, boo and oh!

Now that we have a grammar rap, parts of speech will be a snap!

JANICE GASSER

Sentence Rummy

Upper-grade students enjoy this playful way to practice sentence building. To make a deck for two to four players, you'll need 60 index cards. On each card write one word, allowing 10 cards for each of the following parts of speech: noun, pronoun, verb, article, adjective, adverb. Placed together, the various cards should create coherent sentences.

To play, each student receives seven cards. The remaining cards are placed facedown. The player to the dealer's right asks another player, "Do you have a _____?" The blank is a part of speech that he or she needs to make a complete sentence. If the other player has the card, he or she must give it away. But if the other player doesn't have the card, the one who did the asking draws from the center pile. A player must wait for his or her next turn before laying down a completed sentence. The first to use all of his or her cards wins.

VERENA CHANCE

Nouns Galore

The familiar yellow school bus is a perfect vehicle for teaching about nouns. Mount a large drawing of a school bus on the bulletin board. Next, divide the students into four teams. Give the first team responsibility for designing highway signs, labeling each sign with a place name, and attaching the signs to the board. Ask the second group to cut from magazines pictures of people and to arrange these as passengers on the bus. The third group locates pictures of items bus riders might take with them and attaches these. The fourth group thinks of abstract ideas for slogans, stickers, or banners. Kids write these in varied letter styles, highlight with markers, cut out, and attach to the body of the bus. The finished display illustrates four categories of nouns — places, people, things, and ideas.

SANDRA MORIARTY

Parts of Speech

Prepville

Reinforce the idea of prepositions with this project. Ask students to cut prepositions from advertisements. Students then construct a "city" with the advertisements on a blank bulletin board. The project not only requires knowledge of prepositions, but also working together as a class and planning in advance. CAROL REHM

Arty Adjectives

Include this creative word-play exercise when studying adjectives. First, have students choose an adjective and define it by drawing the word in such a way that it reflects its definition. (For example, the word "fat" might be written in large, puffy letters; sour might contain a lemon-shaped o.) Students then use a dictionary to find synonyms and antonyms for their classmates' word-drawings. Attach the drawings to the bulletin board, then have students use the drawings to write paragraphs. After the paragraphs have been edited and rewritten, bind them into a class booklet and display. LINDA DEITCHMAN

Vacation With Adjectives

Give students practice using descriptive language with this travel brochure activity. To begin, show kids sample brochures from a local travel agent. Point out examples of adjectives used to describe vacation spots. Then ask kids to design their own travel brochure, using vivid adjectives to describe a real or imaginary place. Accompanying illustrations can be drawn or cut from magazines. DAVID APPLEBY

Grammar Onstage

Looking for a new way to teach parts of speech? Try theatrics! Team up kids in groups of three or four and ask each group to pick a different part of speech as the subject of a presentation before the rest of the class. Each group creates a three-to-five-minute skit about its word class. Skits should include a definition, examples, and proper visuals that help illustrate the part of speech. Be sure to plan for rehearsal time. You may even want to schedule encore performances as a means of review! MARY BRITTON-SIMMONS

Punctuation

The Daily Paragraph

To reinforce grammar skills, I've incorporated a valuable learning activity into the curriculum that I call The Daily Paragraph. Every morning, I write a paragraph on the board without punctuation and capitalization. I then ask students to copy the paragraph and add the correct punctuation.

Here's the twist: The main subject of The Daily Paragraph is Rodon, an imaginary creature from a planet in a faraway galaxy. Rodon paragraphs are a fun relief from the usual, somewhat dry, paragraphs I'd been using from my students' grammar books. Rodon is a curious creature who loves visiting the planet earth. He has a "brainometer" with which to do his homework and a "planet hopper" in which to go to school. My fourth graders are captivated by Rodon! I encourage them to accompany their revised paragraphs with lively illustrations. We also use Rodon as a springboard for creative writing. For instance, children describe other gadgets Rodon might use in his daily activities. Try creating your own classroom character — and let the writing begin.   PEGGY LEWIS

Puzzling Punctuation

Divide the class into teams of three or four students each. Write a sentence that contains numerous errors in punctuation and capitalization on the board. Then have each team send a team member to the board to correct one error. If the student correctly fixes the grammatical error and can give the reason for the correction, such as "Contractions take an apostrophe" or "Abbreviations begin with a capital letter," his or her team earns a point. Each team rotates players. The team who achieves the highest score by the end of the game wins.
BARBARA LASSMAN

Punctuation Punch

Learn how well your students are grasping punctuation with an extra game the next time you write sentences on the board. Omit the punctuation marks and ask students to supply them without speaking. Define a set of symbols to represent punctuation marks. Raised hands could indicate question marks, clapping makes the point for exclamations, stomp feet once for periods and sigh for commas.   SANDRA GOODMAN

If Animals Could Talk

Have students clip pictures of animals from magazines, then choose two or three favorites and affix them to a piece of paper. Ask students to compose a dialogue between the animals, using proper punctuation and paragraph form. Encourage children to make the stories as kooky or as serious as they'd like. Display the finished stories in your classroom.   RENA ALLEN

Penmanship

Cursive Kingdom

Turn your classroom into an imaginary "cursive kingdom." Combine handwriting practice with activities that relate to fairy tale themes. Here are ideas to get you started.

Charter member: List kingdom (handwriting) rules and a motto on a sheet of bulletin board paper. Trace a line for each student's name and tear the edges for an aged effect. Ask the kids to take turns using a quill pen to sign their names on the "charter."

Knightly news: Give kids examples of headlines: "Prince Locates Glass Slipper," "Dragons Found Lurking in Dungeons," "Unicorn Sightings Reported." Then ask each child to write a brief news article for a handwritten class newspaper.

The Princess and the pen: To emphasize slant, size, shape, and neatness, prepare four samples in your own handwriting, with one main error in each. Across from the samples, write the names of four princesses: Slantissa, Sizella, Shapetta, and Sloppyanna. Laminate the samples and give one to each student. Kids circle the errors in each sample, then draw a line from each example to the princess who wrote it.
SYLVIA FOUST

Once upon a time there was a frog named Dan. He was very green and....

Cursive Writing Aid

One of the problems children often face when learning cursive writing is positioning the paper at the correct angle. Clipboards may help.

Have students place clipboards straight in front of them. Then have them place their papers in the most comfortable position for writing. When they find the position that is best for them, attach the paper to the clipboard at that angle. With a marker, draw a line on the clipboard to indicate the preferred angle. Have students use this technique for other class work, not just for the handwriting practice. Soon they will automatically place their papers at this angle without the aid of the clipboard.
JULIA FREEMAN

Handwriting Helper

For practice that saves paper, create a handwriting aid using contact paper, liquid shoe polish, and cotton swabs. First, cover an old desktop with solid-color contact paper. Next, make dot-to-dot letters and numerals on the paper using white liquid shoe polish and a swab. Add green food coloring to the polish for marking the starting point of each character. A child connects the dots with chalk to practice letter or numeral formation, then erases his or her work to prepare for the next student.
JUDIANN DERHAKE

Spelling

Magnetic ABCs

Liven up a spelling lesson with the aid of magnetic alphabet letters, available at most toy stores.

Divide the class in half and give each side two complete alphabet sets. Then have each team randomly distribute five or six letters to each team member. Have members of each team sit in a row. The team member at the beginning of each row stands. Now call out a spelling word. Any team member who has a letter (or letters) in the given word immediately passes the letter along the row until it reaches the student who is standing. The student up "at bat" quickly arranges the letters on his or her side of the blackboard to spell the word correctly.

The first team to arrange the letters in the correct spelling order receives two points. The second team receives one point if they also spell the word correctly. Students take turns at the board. The team with the highest score at the end of the game is the winner.

MARGARET HOAGLAND

Spunky Spelling

Put some spunk into spelling with these activities.

• Make a "Refrigerator List." Each time you introduce a new list of spelling words, have students copy the words in their best handwriting, proofread their lists, and mount them on construction paper. The lists go home to be placed on refrigerator doors, where parents and students have them handy for quick study and practice.

• Give students a sheet of art paper each. Have them choose a colored pencil to go with each spelling word and write each word as many times as they wish in a pleasing pattern.

• Give each student a 3-foot length of ribbon, yarn, or crepe paper. Dictate the spelling words and have students spell them out loud as they "write" the letters in the air with large arm movements. Try this as a playground or physical education activity.   LINDA EISENTROUT

Spelling Sidetrips

Give students out-of-text experiences with these snappy spelling reinforcers.

Cutout. Each child writes his or her spelling words on a sheet of paper, then cuts letters, parts of words, or entire words from magazines and newspapers to duplicate the list.

Hop-out. Use masking tape to create an alphabet grid on the floor. Kids hop on the grid, calling out letters to spell each list word.

Tile-out. Working in teams of two, kids use letter tiles from board games like Scrabble to practice spelling. One partner chooses a list word, drops appropriate letters into a bag, then empties the tiles onto a desktop. The other child unscrambles the letters to spell the word.

Look-out. Ask each student to look through old magazines for pictures that illustrate spelling list words. For example, if the spelling word is surprise, he or she may find a picture of a child opening a present. Kids cut out pictures and paste them to notebook paper. For each picture, students write the word in a sentence.

TOM BERNAGOZZI

Spelling

Define-O

Try this variation on Bingo to reinforce spelling. Distribute rectangular pieces of tagboard and have students draw two lines horizontally and two lines vertically, creating nine boxes in all. Instruct students to write "Define-O" at the top of their game cards, then write a different word from the week's spelling list in each box, except for the center one, which is a free space.

To play the game, stand at the front of the classroom and call out one word definition at a time. When a pupil's card contains the word that matches the definition, he or she covers the space with a small square of paper. The first child to cover three spaces horizontally, vertically, or diagonally calls out "Define-O," and wins the game. As a prize, the winner may call out the definitions for the next round.
REBECCA WEBSTER GRAVES

The World Famous Spelling Box

Have you ever given a spelling test and two weeks later the students seem to have forgotten the words? Do you need a spelling aid that increases students' spelling ability across the curriculum? If so, then meet "The World Famous Spelling Box."

Divide the class into pairs. Each pair will receive one box. The box can be a cereal or shoe box. The pairs name and decorate their boxes. They cut a hole in the top of the box wide enough for access. Then explain the following rules to the class:

After each spelling pretest, each pair of students will copy each of the weekly words onto small slips of paper.

Pairs of students will place the slips of paper in their boxes.

Whenever a special word from another subject area (such as science, social studies, math, etc.) catches students' eyes, they are to write it on a slip of paper and place it in their boxes.

Assign students to use the boxes one or twice a week for 30 minutes. Students must draw a slip of paper from the box, look at the word, say it, then close their eyes and spell the word. After spelling the word, they must check and see if they spelled it correctly. If not, students start again.

Use your imagination and invent some fun spelling games to use with the spelling boxes as well as spelling drills.
BONNIE WALKER

Wet Letter Days

Kids who can't resist writing on steamy windows will want to try this review activity. Call student volunteers to dip a finger in a glass of water and to write spelling or vocabulary words on the chalkboard. Others can quickly try to decipher each word before it evaporates.
BERNICE WHITE

Wheel Of Fortune

Learning spelling and vocabulary words can be made fun by playing a version of "Wheel of Fortune." Slashes are drawn on the chalkboard for each letter in a word. Children take turns guessing letters, while a student writes the correct letters in the proper spaces on the board.

Children are taught to look for blends, suffixes and vowels to reinforce spelling strategies. Small rewards are given to the children for correctly guessing a word.
VALERIE DAVIS

Spelling

Spelling By Committee

Try basing weekly spelling lists on word banks you and your class create rather than on lists in workbooks.

Select Categories

First, decide on relevant categories for the banks. A good start might be your school and community — the names of your school and staff, students' names, community landmarks and officials. Other possible categories? Try a bank of newspaper words like scoop, byline, investigation — plus places in the news and words from the travel section and from special features. You'll find a bankload of words in student textbooks. Alternate between language arts, math, social studies, and science. You might even tap physical education or sports rules. Consider words connected with holidays and names of religions and cultures. Try words related to kids' hobbies, words associated with grocery shopping, words you might use on a camping trip. Word-bank categories for younger children might include colors, numbers, animals, and toys. You might even include a word or two from your spelling book!

Change the Week

Next, change your spelling week so that new words are introduced on Wednesday and tested on the following Tuesday. In many schools, the highest number of absences occur on Mondays or Fridays. This new week should help eliminate frequent cries of, "I wasn't here on Monday, so I should have an extra day to study," or "I need a makeup test."

Choose a Committee

Appoint a rotating committee to help you choose each week's words. On Monday morning, tell the committee the word-bank category for the week. Pick 10 words yourself, and ask the committee to choose the other 10 by Wednesday morning. Wednesday afternoon present the list to the whole class.

Create Projects

Require a certain number of completed exercises for each lesson. Give everyone a master list of exercises to choose from and post an enlarged version on a bulletin board. Here are some examples: Make a word search and have another student complete it. Divide the words into syllables. Write each word along with a simple definition. Use all the words to form a picture. Write each word five times. Use each word in a sentence. Scramble the words and ask another student to unscramble them. Use your list to make a crossword puzzle. Write a short story and underline each spelling word.

Test on Tuesday

After Tuesday's test, ask kids to use words they missed in an exercise, spelling each word at least five times. This is due by the end of the day and closes each spelling week.

Though teaching spelling without a workbook is a bit more work for you, it's worth it. Kids enjoy being on the committee to choose the words of the week or to come up with categories for new banks. You'll still need to help tailor lists according to grade level and to make sure basic spelling rules are covered. But you'll also find that students are excited to learn a variety of words that have real meaning for them.

SALLY KRAUSE

Take Time For Spelling

Give students large, blank wrist watches made from construction paper. Students decorate face and band, without putting numbers on the face. Hang watches on bulletin board. Each week as students master their spelling words, they earn a number to put on their watch faces. Numbers can be press-on or written on with a permanent marker. Add cardboard or paper hands after all numbers are earned.   SUE KREIBICH

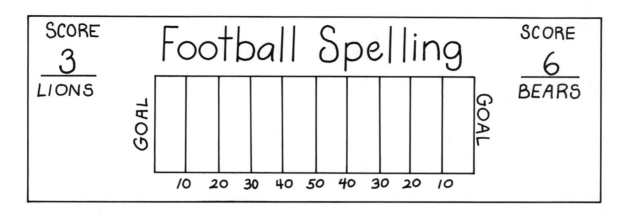

Spelling Scoreboard

Draw a football field like the one pictured. Divide the class into two teams and give each a few minutes to choose a team name. Put the names on the board and you're ready for the kickoff!

Flip a coin to see which team will go first. Give the first team a word to spell and let members huddle for a predetermined amount of time (30 seconds). Then one of the team members must spell the word. If the word is spelled correctly, put a check beside the 10-yard line. Play continues until the first team misses a word or reaches its own 10-yard line. When a team reaches its own 10-yard line, the next word is worth six points.

At this point, the team has 10 seconds to huddle and decide if it wants a hard word or an easy one. One child, without help from the others, must spell the word. A hard word is worth two points for the conversion. An easy word is worth only one for the kick. One way to differentiate between hard and easy words is to say that an easy word is one that's been on a previous spelling list. A hard word is one that students haven't had yet.

If a team misses a word, it has to "turn over the ball" to the other team, which starts from the 10-yard line on the opposite side.

To add a little strategy to the game, let each team call time-out and go into a huddle to decide if it wants to stop its procession down the field and go for a field goal, that is, spell a word for three points and then turn the ball over. Allow only three time-outs per half. Set a penalty of 10 yards for being in a huddle too long. Make sure you set a time limit for the length of your game before you begin.

PAUL SIKORA

Reinforce Spelling Skills With Sign Language

Here is a way to integrate a multisensory approach to learning spelling. Teach the class the correct way to finger spell.

Each week ask students to finger spell words from the spelling list on their hands.

Ask students to watch others make their words and try to read them. Students take turns making the words for others to read, reinforcing their learning.

Adding the kinesthetic/tactile method of learning reinforces the lesson with students who do not perform well in the visual and auditory modes of learning. Finger spelling allows students to "make" letters on their hands, incorporating a tactile approach to spelling.

Finger spelling also allows for positive reinforcement as the whole class pulls together to learn something new.

VALERIA HAMRICK

Picture Story

Increase your storytelling powers and kids' imaginative and listening skills with this picture technique. Cover a large picture with a sheet of construction paper in which you have cut windows. As you describe the details of a setting, a character, or an event, open these windows to reveal only the portion of the hidden picture you are describing. Number each window flap so you'll open them in the correct order. After the description is complete, remove the covering sheet of construction paper to reveal the entire picture.

JANE PRIEWE

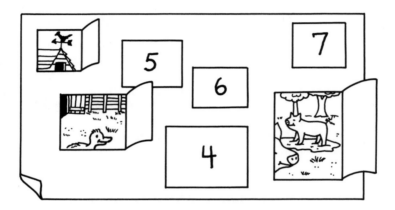

Anybody Listening?

Test the listening skills of upper-grade kids with some lined paper and the following oral directions.
• Start at the top of your paper and make the largest square your paper allows.
• Divide your square into three equal parts with horizontal lines.
• Divide your square into three equal parts vertically.
• Number each box with small numerals beginning in the top left box.
• Place an exclamation mark in the box with the highest numeral.
• If you have nine boxes, print the word "wonderfully" in the center of box eight.
• If you have more than nine boxes, print the word "better" in box eight.
• Print the word "listen" in box five.
• If your numerals are large, print "you'd" in box one.
• If your numerals are small, print "you" in box four.
• If all directions are followed, the student ends up with the message — You listen wonderfully!

CAROL WAHLENMAYER

Listening Tips

Origami As A Creative Listening Tool

 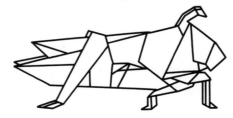

Origami can help students develop good listening skills if the folds are learned in an organized fashion.

Students keep their eyes on the teacher, who demonstrates one fold at a time. Students make the fold at their seats. To signify they are ready to proceed, students put their hands in their laps after they finish. They raise their hands if they are having trouble, helping the teacher to find those who are having difficulties. When all the students are done, the class proceeds to the next fold.

Origami also helps maintain discipline. If this activity is engaged in early in the year, students develop listening skills at the beginning of the year, and kids who are tempted to be silly or daydream don't have the chance.

Origami not only aids the teacher in maintaining discipline in the classroom, but it also can be integrated into the art curriculum throughout the entire school year. Three-D designs, origami sculptures, jewelry, rings, storage containers, collages, flowers, animals, paper dolls, Christmas ornaments and other decorative seasonal items are just a few of the many things that your students can make using this ancient Japanese art.

LINDA YOFFE

Try Whispering

Improve students' listening skills with a new twist on the old game, "Simon Says." Instead of speaking the commands in a normal voice, whisper them. This is also a great way to slow down the pace of a game while capturing the children's attention.

ANNE PACHECO

Listening

Listening Activity

Try this activity to hone students' listening skills. This activity lends itself to rainy days. Divide the class into three groups and assign each group a number from one to three. Tell the students you are going to read them a poem and they should listen for instructions and do as they are told. The poem may be read or chanted to a hoe-down beat.

Listening Poem

The 1's stand up,
And the 1's sit down.
The 2's stand up and spin around.
The 3's stand up and do the same.
Please sit down when I call your group's name.
3's — 2's
Now it's time for the 1's again,
So please stand up and reach for the sky.
Reach so ever, ever high
And sit down, 1's, when you hear me sigh.
OK, 3's, up on your toes
And put your hand upon your nose
And would you also touch your toes?
Now stand back up and spin around
And do that 'til I say, 3's sit down.
"Sigh."
Stand up, 2's, don't sit around.
Jog in place with your hands on your hips
And while you're at it, pucker your lips.
1's stand and 3's sit down.

1's look at your neighbor and shake his hand.
Shake it 'til it turns to sand.
OK, 2's, I've seen enough, sit back down
So the 3's can stand up.
Now what, oh, what, can I have the 3's do?
I think I'd like to hear them moo.
That's good, 3's, now stop that moo
And hold up your fingers and show me 2.
OK, 1's, you can stop your shaking
And 1's can sit down, and so can the 3's.
Now everyone is sitting down,
And that makes the teacher wear a frown.
So the 3's stand up
And the 1's stand up
And the 3's sit down.
1's, please start to spin around.
Now 3's, stand up and start to spin
And the 2's can also start to spin
1's can stop
So can the 2's and 3's.
All groups sit down, would you please?

ANNA ALLEN

Speaking

Experts In The Class

Every student in your classroom is an expert on something. Students have hobbies, participate in sports, collect stamps, listen to music, and belong to special clubs.

Ask your students to define their interests and hobbies to determine an area in which they are an expert. Have students determine what their hobbies and interests are, where and to whom they could go for more information on that topic, and what subjects they would like to know more about.

After the students choose a subject, they are assigned to research their topic. They present their findings in a five-minute oral report. Make sure to leave time for a question and answer period. The whole class learns from the resident "experts."　　　　　　　　MELANIE VICKERS

Calling For Help

Many children know the number to call for emergency services, but few know how to give the proper information needed to obtain help as quickly as possible.

Be sure all of your students know the emergency number. Then role play and allow students to practice giving vital information on a play telephone. While the teacher plays the operator, have the children practice the following:
• Say "This is an emergency."
• Tell what happened.
• Tell where it happened.
• Tell when it happened.
• Give your name and the victim's name.
• Don't hang up. The operator may need more information or give advice.

As the children practice, remind them not to play on the phone at home.　　CARLYN ROEDELL

Reading Celebrity For A Day

Give your students the opportunity to be celebrities. Ask individual children to be a reader for an afternoon. A reader chooses pieces of his or her own writing to share with the class and other guests. The student designs and mails invitations to each special guest (relatives, friends, school staff, students from other classrooms, news reporters), inviting each to attend the reading.

After writing introductions for each piece, practicing the oral presentations and planning the menu for the reception following the reading, the student is ready to appear before the audience. A video camera provides an even greater audience as children can share their special tape with friends and family who were unable to come.
KATHY KELLY

Becoming Better Communicators

Help pupils become better communicators with this activity involving partners. Two sets of seven different colored sticks are given to each pair of children — tongue depressors colored with magic markers work nicely. The amount and type of materials will vary with availability and grade level.

Partner One arranges the sticks in a pattern that Partner Two cannot see. Then Partner Two tries to replicate the pattern by listening to the first child's description and by asking the first child questions. After five minutes, let the partners compare patterns. Assess the success of various question-asking and information-giving strategies with the entire group.

The game can then be repeated with Partner Two constructing a pattern. You may want to set the condition that Partner One cannot start building until all question asking and information giving is completed. The extra challenge of paying close attention and remembering instructions is added. After five minutes, the class should again assess the successful and less successful communication skills employed.
ANNE SCHREIBER

Observing and Remembering

Tracks and Trails

Turn kids into trackers for an outdoor adventure that builds observation skills.

On city lots or in country woods, a light covering of freshly fallen snow should leave evidence of a variety of activity. Ask students to look for animal tracks and to hypothesize about what made them. For example, cat prints are smaller, rounder, and closer together than dog prints. Tracks that seem to end at trees may suggest squirrels. A tail print following a set of tiny tracks was likely left by a rat or mouse.

Extend observations to include signs of people too — marks from a garbage can, ski trails, and shoe prints. Ask kids to figure out as much as they can about the person who made each set of tracks by looking for clues such as type of shoe and length of stride. Challenge students to find their own tracks on the return to school.

Back in the classroom, ask your students to write a creative story, poem, or script for a play about the person or creature that made one of the tracks they observed. Students might also enjoy illustrating their stories with chalk drawings for a showy, snowy finish.

NINA SALAMON

Detail Detectives

Boost kids' observation skills by asking them to recall details about a picture, person, or place they've recently seen. Here are some ideas to get you started:

• Ask students to tell you what they see from the cafeteria (or other room) windows.

• Give kids a quick look at a map of your state or the United States then ask them to draw its shape. How much more detail do they show as the year progresses?

• Give kids a ten-second glance at a picture or advertisement from a magazine, then put it away. What do they remember about it?

• Have students close their eyes. How many can tell you what the person next to them is wearing? Who knows what is on the walls of the classroom?

• Ask for four or five volunteers to line up in front of the class and assume a position; for example: back to the class, crouched, hands on hips. Have them hold the pose for five seconds, then relax. Who can return each volunteer to the original pose?

JOAN NOVELLI

Observing and Remembering

Windows On The World

Improve your students' observation skills with this activity that capitalizes on the changeable winter weather. Start by drawing four different windows on a blank sheet of paper. Label the windows morning, noon, evening, and night and make enough copies of the activity sheet for every student in your class. Wait for a day on which the weather forecasters predict snow or rain. Then distribute the worksheet and ask students to observe the world outside their windows at four different times during the day. Students should record their observations on the corresponding windows. Encourage kids to look for different colors, textures, and objects. They can record sounds and smells, too.

PAULA MILLENDER GOINES

Mag Flaps

Strengthen students' observation and memory skills by creating a supply of magazine learning aids.

Cut out a magazine picture and glue it to the top half of a sheet of oaktag. Fold a second oaktag sheet of the same size in half and glue it to the bottom of the first piece so that the magazine picture shows. Lift up the folded flap of the plain oaktag and write questions about the picture. Refold the flap to conceal the questions. Students study the picture, then lift up the flap and cover the picture and read the questions. Kids write answers on scrap paper and check them against the picture when finished.

LINDA MARTIN MERCER

Memory Walk

Try this activity to help your students use their powers of observation and memory of detail. Take them on a walk around the school and surrounding grounds. Explain it is important not to talk so everyone can concentrate on listening and looking.

During the walk, the teacher will need to concentrate, too, for preparation of the follow-up activities.

When you return to the classroom, ask the children some specific questions about what they saw and heard. Have them write down their answers on a piece of paper. Then discuss the answers with the class, remembering different answers to the same question can be correct. End the lesson with a discussion about why it is important to look, listen and observe the world around us.

LEE DIGIANO

Creative Thinking

Fire Up Those Brain Cells

Use these brainstorming ideas to develop some creative thinking techniques. Ask pupils to call out every red object they know. When they have achieved a lengthy list, tell them that they have just brainstormed. Ask them to close their eyes and imagine what it would look like to have storms occur inside their brains. Once they have this visual image, enumerate the rules of brainstorming: try to produce a lot of ideas; make these ideas unusual; build upon each other's ideas; defer judgment during the process.

Divide the children into small groups and display a hockey puck. Explain that the gym teacher has received 500 hockey pucks that are too small to use for hockey. Their job is to produce a list of all possible uses for the hockey pucks. Share some of the more unusual ideas with the class.

"Peephole" magazine photographs (pictures almost entirely covered by blank paper, with only a small segment of the photograph showing) encourage students to explore all possible explanations of the content of the photograph.

Distribute colored paper on which three simple shapes are drawn. Ask the children to brainstorm what these shapes could become if they could cut them out and move them anywhere they'd like on a blank piece of paper. After the brainstorming session, have children glue the shapes to the blank paper, and complete their work by adding crayon to their products.

Have pupils design a new animal, giving various environmental conditions. Begin by comparing animals' physical characteristics and habits with their environments. Generate a long list of examples, thereby involving brainstorming in the lesson. Divide the class into groups of three and give each group a set of environmental conditions. Their task is to draw and label an imaginary animal that would suit the environmental conditions given. The groups are also instructed to list pertinent survival information, such as diet and social habits. Compare the groups' creations. This activity is useful as a creative writing starter as well.

Ask children to prioritize items for survival. First discuss what household items children feel are vital. Naturally, there will be a wide difference of opinion on this subject. Then break the class into groups of five and ask them to imagine that they are going to a desert island and can only bring five items with them. They have to choose which five items are most important for their survival, out of the 10 items you provide. Your list will vary somewhat with grade level. You may include items such as a television set, pens, paper, a candle, matches, a computer, markers, a supply of food, a supply of water, a cooking pot, a sleeping bag, a house, a bicycle, skis, rope, soap, games, books, a pocket knife, candy, and shoes. When your class has completed designing their lists, each group should explain their rationale to the rest of the class. ANNE SCHREIBER

Dictionary and Other Reference Books

Dictionary Guide Words

Help your students learn to use dictionary guide words with this simple activity. Label two kids as "guide" words. Have them stand at the front of the room, several feet apart. Give pieces of paper with words on them to all students. Have students arrange themselves in alphabetical order between the two guide words.

Students have a great time positioning themselves in the correct order, as if they themselves were words in the dictionary.

GERRI L. LEAKE

Dictionary Game

One student looks up a word in the dictionary that other students are unfamiliar with . Then, the rest of the class writes what they think the definition of the word is in dictionary-style format.

After the students have written their definitions, they turn in their papers to the teacher. The teacher then reads the definition to the class. The students guess which definition is closest to the correct definition. The student who guesses correctly earns bonus points.

Students learn quickly to write definitions dictionary style, and the game builds vocabulary.

NICK SMITH

Dictionary Markings

Introduce the standard pronunciation symbols used in students' dictionaries. Then challenge kids to look up words and write corresponding dictionary spellings to make traffic signs, warning labels, and messages for others to read.

GENEVIEVE BYLINOWSKI

Stumpers

Stock bookshelves with almanacs, record books, atlases, and other reference books. Ask students to use these sources to find information for questions that fit categories you've listed on the board. Students submit questions to you to place on the proper tree stump. You can keep the answers at your desk or hide them underneath the stumps. Vary the categories weekly and give out "We Couldn't Stump You" awards.

SUE KREBICH

Dictionary Hunt

Give students practice with dictionary and vocabulary skills. Each day, write a letter and a topic on the chalkboard — M-something made from metal, C-something found in cities, B-a kind of bird. Then invite students to think of an appropriate word, to locate it in the dictionary, and to write it on the board.

HELEN THOMAS

The Writing Process

Chart A Course To Great Reports

By focusing on the writing process and identifying the steps involved in developing a research paper, elementary students can easily complete long reports over a four-to-five-week period. Choose a time of year when the project will not be undermined by holidays or other special projects. Make sure other classes will not be competing for library reference materials. You may wish to display papers done by last year's students to show that the project is appropriate for them.

Then explain the project and discuss briefly the steps they will take: deciding on a topic; searching out facts and ideas; organizing note cards and making outlines; selecting, rearranging, and combining information and ideas; reflecting on what worked and what didn't. Distribute manila envelopes to hold all materials they will collect — note cards, outlines, and so on — and the progress chart they will complete (see reproducible on page 47).

Arrange for a trip to the library for students to choose a topic. (Do not choose one for those persons who are undecided, but suggest ideas if necessary.) Assist in selecting reference materials. As pupils decide on a topic and the references they will use, complete that part of the progress chart.

The next challenge is note-taking. Help them be selective by suggesting subtopics to put at the top of cards. Show how to include only key words and phrases on the cards by helping them identify what's essential.

Then guide children as they put their note cards in order so that facts and ideas begin to form a logical flow. You might ask them to imagine that they know nothing at all about their topic. What would they like to know most? What kinds of facts and ideas would keep their attention? What's the best way to end a report — summary, observation, incredible fact?

Once children have placed the facts and ideas from a few cards into an outline, take a look and alert them to any obvious gaps in information or logic.

As they write their first drafts, encourage pupils to expand on the outline in their own words. Then edit these drafts yourself and discuss changes and suggestions with each child. Remind them that final drafts should incorporate these revisions.

When students have written and proofread their final drafts, they are ready to assemble it with other components — pictures (handdrawn or from magazines), a bibliography, and a cover.

Evaluate the completed reports by discussing the process. What were the obstacles students encountered? How did they manage their time outside the classroom? What could they have done to make the research and writing process smoother and more enjoyable? Help them to realize that following each step in the writing process makes preparing long reports a very doable project.   JOAN DANIELS CAMPBELL

Take A Look At Our Book

Bring a blank-page hardcover book to class. Tell students that they are going to write and illustrate a real book together as a class. Designate one student the "keeper" of the book. Then have children volunteer to undertake various functions in the book-making process, such as creating a book jacket, title page, dedication, table of contents, and so on. Fill the pages of the book with students' creative writing assignments, poems, drawings, math teasers, photographs, and other creative expressions that exemplify their personalities. When the book is finished, ask your school librarian to place it in the library's permanent collection.
KEN BIERLY

NAME: _____

Progress Chart
for research paper on _____
_____

Tasks	Due Date	Teacher's Comments	Teacher's Initials	Parent's Initials
Topic and References Chosen				
Note Cards				
Outline				
First Draft				
Final Draft				
Visuals Bibliography Cover				
Finished Report				

Story Starters

Story Seeds

Invite students to become "budding authors" with this creative writing assignment. Ask kids to choose one of these titles: The Money Plant, The Seeds That Brought Rainbows, The Cow That Ate The Golden Seeds, The Crying Tree, The Plant That Came To Dinner, or The Kissing Flower. Each child completes a story, then makes a plant like that described in the story using construction paper, scissors, and glue. Display stories and plants on a bulletin board titled: These Stories Will Grow On You! Just see what stems from this activity.

REBECCA FRIARY

Communication With Big Feet

Encourage communication with an unusual conversation starter. Beg or borrow a pair of huge shoes (size 16, bright and colorful preferred). Search the school for someone to fill them. Chances are you'll fail but students will increase communication along the way.

Start the search in class. Encourage suggestions as to who would wear the shoes. Try them on. Take pictures. Write stories about them. Post stories and pictures outside the classroom to involve and arouse questions from other classes.

Target cooperative staff members to visit. Try on the shoes. Again, take pictures, write stories, share experiences outside the classroom.

A "footnote" to the project might be a story about the children's own shoes, from the shoe's point of view.

DELORES CAMILOTTO

Alphabooks

Add a twist to writing assignments by using the "ABC formula." Kids create stories with 26 sentences only. The first sentence starts with A, the second with B, and so on down to Z. Mystery and adventure stories work best with the formula, and are as easy to write as A-B-C.

LINDA WHITAKER

What's Inside The Mystery Box?

To introduce creative writing to my first-graders, I came up with the following idea.

Find a box that's large enough to hold one of a variety of items, such as a teddy bear, a pine cone, a tennis ball, and so on. Then make a hole in the box to accommodate a small hand. Each morning, place a different item into the box. Then during your class' writing period, ask each child to go to the Mystery Box, feel the item found inside, and write a short description of what he or she thinks the item might be. After students have finished their stories, have them share their guesses with the class. As a final exercise, reveal the contents of the box and ask children to list adjectives for further describing the mystery object.

VIRGINIA B. JACKSON

Story Starters

Mini Stories

To help teach pupils about sentences, paragraphs, and creative writing, have them create mini stories to save and reread throughout the school year. Here's how:

Write sets of three questions, each set on a specific topic, such as pets, sports, food, and so on. For example:

1. What is your favorite sport?
2. With whom do you play this sport?
3. When do you play this sport?

Assign the questions as homework, one Monday, one Tuesday, and one Wednesday. Students should answer each question with a complete sentence. Each morning, check to see that the sentences relate to the question. For homework on Thursday night, the pupils create a title and recopy their answers in paragraph form by indenting the first line. Each pupil now has a mini story with a title, main idea, and details. The story is then put in the pupil's folder so at the end of the year the folder is filled with mini stories that are fun to read.

LOIS WAXMAN

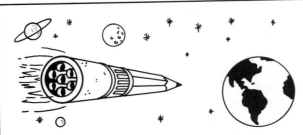

Mission: Blast-Off!

This fun-filled "space mission" in creative writing correlates with a unit on space travel. To set the stage, dim the lights in your classroom and play an appropriate record for background music such as the soundtrack from "Aliens" or "2001: A Space Odyssey." Then tell students they're about to board a rocket ship from Mars to Earth. Have them sit quietly in their seats and imagine a fabulous journey through space. After a few minutes, give each child a specific mission written on a paper rocket. One might be, "Visit a zoo on Earth and describe it to your Martian friends back home." The student must then create a story about how a zoo would appear to a Martian. Other missions might include explaining a supermarket or describing a television set. Turn the lights back on and have students complete their assignments before returning to Mars. To make this project even more exciting, you may want to construct a simple control panel from heavy cardboard, paint, wood, and a set of twinkling holiday lights, and place the creation on your desk. Get set for some space-age fun.

LEE ANN PENKALA

Fun With Fairy Tales

As a light-hearted, end-of-the-year writing activity that also reinforces sequencing skills, have your class modernize traditional fairy tales and present them to the class.

First choose a familiar tale, such as "Cinderella," and read it aloud to the class. Next, have students share ideas on how they would write a modern version of "Cinderella" — perhaps by substituting a sneaker for a glass slipper, a Ferrari for a coach, and so on. Then outline the plot of the story on the chalkboard, using the students' ideas as a guide. This will help them write and illustrate their own modern versions of the tale. After students have completed their writing assignments, encourage them to share their stories and illustrations with the class.

PAMELA MINSHELL

Story Starters

Label Writing

Ask students to collect empty plastic or cardboard containers at home. Glue bottles, paste jars, salad dressing bottles, medicine containers, fruit juice boxes, mouthwash containers or toothpaste dispensers can all be used. Students should soak the containers in warm water and peel the directions off the back of the container. They should not remove the front label identifying the product.

Students then bring the containers to school, and during creative writing time, write directions for the container labels. Have them glue their labels on the backs of their containers.

Display the containers in a special area of the classroom titled "Our Writing Store."
PAULA MILLENDER GOINES

Writing Motivators

Spark kids' creativity with these imaginative motivators.
• Prepare an "idea bag" for each student. Place an object or two in a small paper bag and twist shut. Suggested items: a rusty old key, a broken doll, an airline ticket. Just for fun, give students a minute to exchange bags sight unseen, and then ask each student to write a short story about the contents.
• Paste onto index cards pictures of inanimate objects cut from toy catalogs and magazines. Place the cards upside down on a table, and ask each student to select one. Tell kids to imagine that each card just started talking about itself. Every child writes a story about what his or her card says.

• Write the names of uncommon animals — prairie dog, peacock, armadillo — on small sheets of paper. Each student selects one and keeps the animal a secret. After doing some research, each student writes a riddle, poem, or informative paragraph about the animal, reads it to the class, and asks other students to guess the identity.
• Distribute sheets of paper and ask each child to create a title and one-page beginning to a story. The next day, students swap papers to write the second page to each story. The third day, still another student concludes the story with page three. Hold a class sharing session.
JEAN STANGL

Story Cans

To reinforce the concept of elaboration, try this story-building idea. You'll need the following materials: four empty, one-pound coffee cans with plastic lids and about 100 slips of paper. First, draw and cut out a star shape (large enough for a child's hand to fit through) from each lid. Then label the cans *Character, Trait, Location,* and *Problem.* Beginning with the Character can, label the first 25 slips of paper with names of characters. You may take the names from literature

or history, make them up, or use professions, such as captain, first mate, tennis player, and so on. Place the slips of paper in the can. Label 25 slips of paper for the Traits can (honest, loyal, lovable, silly); the Locations can (the African plains, Cape Horn, the attic, under a rock); and the Problems can (had no water, a tornado was approaching, lost the key, couldn't find the house.) Children then pick one slip of paper from each can and compose a story. KATHY FAGGELLA

Story Starters

Cut A Class Story

Keep on hand several bags full of pictures cut from magazines. Use them to challenge students' creative thinking skills as well as their abilities to expand on thoughts.

Have one student start by pulling a picture out of the bag and beginning a story about it. The next student pulls out a second picture and uses it to continue the first student's story. Students proceed in this manner until it's time for the story to end or be continued another time. As kids select the pictures, display them on a table to provide a visual picture of the story as it unfolds.
JOAN NOVELLI

Rewriting News

Assign intermediate and middle school students to clip and read newspaper articles. Then ask students to rewrite the stories in their own words.

After students have perfected their rewritten news stories, give them the opportunity to be "Dan Rather" for a day. Set aside time for the students to read their rewritten versions aloud. Place a desk facing the class in front of the classroom to be used as a "news anchorperson's" desk. Each student takes a turn reading his or her article at the desk in front of the class as if he or she were delivering the news on television.

After each student finishes reading his or her article, class members critique fluency, delivery, clarity, rate, eye contact, and other forms of nonverbal communication.

This activity helps students improve reading and comprehension skills and knowledge of current events. Students also gain an understanding of public speaking and nonverbal communication.
LOIS GASPARRO

Writing By Design

If you're looking for a fun, quick-as-a-wink writing activity, look no further than your stash of old magazines — and your students' imaginations.

First explain to kids that they are to design an unusual room for a new house. Have children look through the magazines for pictures of wacky, exotic items around which to build ideas for the perfect — and most outlandish — interiors. After they've selected and cut out specific pictures, instruct each child to arrange the cutouts on a large piece of white drawing paper. Encourage students to draw in items that they are unable to find in the magazines. Then have each child write a descriptive paragraph about his or her special room, explaining what makes it unique. Staple the paragraphs to the pictures and display in your classroom.
SAMANTHA GEIST

Picture This

Here's a fun way to help kids brainstorm story ideas for creative writing. First, cut pictures from magazines — cars, people, toys, animals, buildings — and paste them on separate index cards. Place cards in a shallow box, then divide the class into groups of four and ask each child in the group to draw a card. Challenge each group to combine the characters or objects on the group's cards in stories written by each student or jointly by each group.
DOROTHY ZJAWIN

More Creative Writing Ideas

Writing Cinquain Poetry

Even primary pupils can create simple, cinquain poetry. Explain that the formula is five lines long — lines one and five have two syllables, line two has four syllables, line three has six, and line four has eight. Each line has a special purpose. The first line is the title or topic of the poem (My Pets). Line two describes the title (Gold, red, yellow). Line three describes an action of the topic (Sparkling in the sunlight). Line four tells of a feeling about the topic (Their sudden movements give me joy). The last line is another word for the title (My Fish).

Have students share their verses. They can write the verse on a shape related to the poem's topic — a fish shape, for example. Then they can paste the shape into a class album or notebook with other verses for classmates to read and enjoy.

Or they can make wall hangers from yarn and five Popsickle sticks. Explain that each student should write one line of his or her verse on each stick. Then they should lay the sticks in order, a half inch apart. Finally, they should turn the sticks over and paste yarn along the two sides, making sure to leave enough length at the top to hang the creation. JANE K. PRIEWE

Fifth Grader For Sale

This creative writing lesson can be used at any grade level. Students pretend they are products that people can purchase and write an advertisement to sell themselves. They may look at other advertisements for samples. Give students these ideas to help them get started:
• List things you can do, such as cleaning windows, tutoring math, telling jokes, scrubbing floors, mowing lawns, cooking breakfast or delivering singing telegrams.
• For how much are you selling?
• What accessories come with you? (Such as a scrub brush and pail, an insect collection, a clown costume, a pet elephant, a maintenance agreement or a lifetime warranty.)
• At what type of store (real and imaginary) can you be found? Discount stores, department stores, dime stores, etc.?
• Let students become as creative and imaginative as possible. Students can also bring pictures of themselves and glue them to the advertisements. Then mount the picture on a cardboard or construction paper base for the teacher to display on a bulletin board. DEANNA KOZUBIK

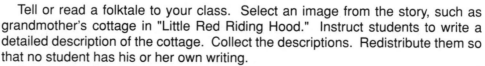

Get The Picture

Tell or read a folktale to your class. Select an image from the story, such as grandmother's cottage in "Little Red Riding Hood." Instruct students to write a detailed description of the cottage. Collect the descriptions. Redistribute them so that no student has his or her own writing.

Each student must attempt to draw the cottage based on the description. No detail can be added to the drawing that isn't included in the description. If artists need more details, they may ask the writers, who must then respond in writing.
CAROLE ANN PIGGINS

Writing Biographies

Time Spirals

Time spirals help students understand that early experiences form the core of their personalities and are never forgotten. Have students draw a spiral in the shape of a snail and divide it into five sections. Each section holds a drawing and a descriptive sentence about an important event in the student's life. The most recent event is pasted on the outermost section; previous events are ordered backward in time toward the center of the spiral. The shape is then cut out and mounted on construction paper of the same shape.

Pairs of students interview each other about an important event in their lives since school started, such as losing their first tooth or learning to ride a bike. Each writes a sentence and draws a picture that illustrates that event and mounts the paper on the outermost section of the spiral.

Students then brainstorm events with adults at home. They select and write a descriptive sentence for three more events. At school, the events are illustrated and pasted in reverse chronological order to the remaining sections of the spiral. With a baby picture as a guide, each student draws his or her baby face and pastes it in the center of the spiral. Using mirrors, each draws a self-portrait and pastes it to the reverse side of the spiral. The spirals are hung with string above the desks of their creators. Students discuss how each personality is unique and how the illustrated events helped form their personalities. KAREN JORGENSEN-ESMAILI

Personal Writing

Encourage students to engage in personal journal writing by asking them to write mini autobiographies. Give students the correct number of index cards to represent each year of their lives. Then, have them take cards home and ask parents, friends, and relatives to help them list interesting events that happened each year. After the students have collected enough information, have them write about their personal experiences in an essay. Not only will this activity get children excited about recording their pasts, but parents, too, will enjoy the personal involvement. TONI HOLLEY

Student Autobiographies

Help students write autobiographies. Divide the project into three time segments: newborn through age 5, ages 6-9, and age 10 to the present. Some students may also want to add a section about their future studies, careers, and personal lives.

Allow the option to focus on one time period in detail so that all students, including adopted or orphaned children, can participate.

Aside from using their memories, students should interview family members, teachers or friends, use family trees, baby books, doctor's records, old photos, family movies and personal artwork to supplement the autobiographies.

The project enhances many basic skills, such as sifting through and choosing research materials, reading and distilling information, organizing notes, proofreading rough drafts and preparing final copy.

Sharing sessions, in which students volunteer details and stories about themselves during the course of the project, enable the children to learn a little more about each other in an entertaining and nonthreatening light. SUSAN GREIF

Letter Writing

Letter Writing Exercise

The following ideas are geared to provide practice in writing thank-you notes.

• Ask students to bring in an unwanted item from home (such as an old golf or tennis ball, an extra piece from a discarded game, empty bandage boxes or a piece of cork). The students wrap these items attractively and attach a gift tag saying who the gift is from. The gifts are then placed in a large box. Each child chooses a gift other than his or her own. The child must then write a sincere thank-you note to the giver for the gift, mentioning in the note specifically how the gift will be used.

• Give each student a strip of paper with a person's name on it and an occasion which would require a thank-you note to be written. Some examples include:

You received a magic kit from your Uncle Max for your birthday.

Your grandfather sent you a dollhouse he made especially for you.

Your grandmother sent you a sleeping bag for Christmas.

After each note has been written, have children design their own unique thank-you cards on which to write their messages.

BARBARA EIDENMULLER

Secret Pals To The Staff

Around holiday time, I encourage my students to show their appreciation for the school staff by making personalized (anonymous) thank-you notes. With my help, each child writes a note to a different staff member, such as the custodian, the secretary, the librarian, the secretary, and so on, without signing his or her name.

After we copy the notes onto holiday stationery and the children decorate them, we attach a treat, such as a baggie full of popcorn, to the notes. Then I pick a couple of "secret elves" to deliver the gifts.

Several days later, the students go in twos to reveal themselves to their pals. My class is delighted with this project, and the staff members get a lift out of it, too!

CHARLOTTE ADELSPERGER

Thank You

It's never too early or too late to teach children to write thank-you notes. Try this fun assignment to help that experience along. Tell children to imagine that they have received a strange and glorious gift. Now they need to write a thank-you note for the gift and also mention how they are going to use it. One example might be thanking someone for a boa constrictor and adding that you can't wait for winter to come so you can use it to keep your neck warm. RHONDA L. ZION

"Time Capsule" Letters

After returning to school from maternity leave, I gave my fifth-grade students a letter-writing assignment that turned out to be a great learning experience. I asked each student to write a "time capsule" letter to my newborn son, Ryan. I told the students that the letters would be put in Ryan's baby book for him to read when he was in the fifth grade.

The students were intrigued by this idea. The assignment was such a success that I have expanded the project. Now, whenever a student in my class has a new sibling arrive into his or her family, we all write "time capsule" letters to the baby. When my students take the letters home, they can feel as if they have added to the specialness of having a newborn in the house.

LAURA KINSEY

Letter Writing

Use Your Thumbs To Make Letter Writing Fun

This stationery-making activity gives letter writing a special luster by combining an art lesson and language arts.

Thumbprint Stationery

You will need:

2 or 3 stamp pads in washable, nontoxic colors

6 pieces of plain paper per student (8 1/2 by 11 for letters, 4 1/4 by 5 1/2 for note paper)

Bright-colored magic markers (Students usually supply)

To begin their designs, students ink their thumbs or fingers on the stamp pads and press them on the paper. They may use one, two or many thumbprints or fingerprints to create a design.

Make a practice sheet of thumbprints so students see different sizes of prints. This helps them decide on their design, think about where the print will appear on the stationery, and give them time to organize their ideas.

After students make their thumbprints, they complete the drawing with colored markers.

Thumbprint designs can express student interest in music, sports, pets, or perhaps a school subject they are studying.

Letters and Notes

To start the letter-writing lesson, you might want to have students think of synonyms for hello and good-bye. Write their suggestions on the chalkboard or a large piece of newsprint.

Discuss types of friendly letters, thank-you notes, birthday greetings, condolences, regrets and so on, to help students think of the type of letter they will write.

You might also ask students if they are familiar with any phrases that appear in each of these letters. Put these on the board too.

As you begin to study the friendly letter form, tell students: "As our bones support the organs of our body, so do the Heading, Greeting (Salutation), Message (Body), Closing and Signature hold a letter or note together."

Give each child a copy of the reproducible on the next page. Use one on the overhead projector as you introduce the parts of a friendly letter.

Heading Ask students to start filling in the lines with their house number and street on the first line. The second line has the city, state, and zip code. The date goes on the third line. Explain that only the date is needed for a note.

Greeting Students can select various greetings for a good friend or acquaintance. Have students select their way of saying "hello" and write it on the appropriate line.

Message Expressing thoughts and feelings in the body of the letter lets students use conceptual thinking, organization, and self-expression skills.

Closing Saying good-bye should be simple. Stress that they should capitalize the first word and use a comma at the end.

Signature The signature appears directly under the closing.

Younger students can cut and paste the words at the bottom of the reproducible onto the form as you talk about each part. As a review, ask older students to identify and write in the parts. Let students use this form to write first drafts of their letters.

While you work with students on their drafts, ask those who are finished to add to the hello and good-bye synonym chart started earlier.

Students should transfer their letters to the stationery they made and put the letters in envelopes; they may then address and mail them.

LOIS PELCARSKY REILLY

Form for letter-writing exercise

Cut out labels below and paste them on boxes provided to identify the parts of a letter.

HEADING

GREETING

CLOSING

MESSAGE

SIGNATURE

The Editing Process

Wandering Editors

Have students make and use "wandering editors" to improve proofreading skills. Give each student a thimble. You can spray paint them, or the children can paint them with acrylics.

Have the children draw faces on the thimbles with colored markers. The thimbles are the students' "wandering editors." Students wear them when they proofread written work.

When a teacher is working one-on-one with a student, she can keep her thimble poised under an error until the student figures out what the mistake was.

CYNTHIA NORBECK

Edit Each Other

Pupils can learn much about the process of writing by working with each other's writing. But often class criticism makes it uncomfortable for the writer. Use this technique to keep the authors anonymous and also to help pupils look for the good points as well as the errors in writing. With a pupil's secret permission, rewrite his or her work on a transparency exactly as the person wrote it, with all misspellings, grammatical errors, and content flaws. Pupils can take turns pointing out any errors, but before making a criticism, he or she must find a good point. "I like the way the writer indented for paragraphs, but there are two words misspelled in the first sentence." Since the writers are not identified unless they want to be, there is no need to be embarrassed by the remarks. And, since the criticizers must also be positive, they must concentrate on the correct points as well as those that are wrong.

Colorful Corrections

When reviewing student compositions, use a color key to highlight specific types of writing errors. For example, use a yellow marker to highlight spelling, orange for capitalization, green for grammatical mistakes. Write explanations in the margin on the same line as the mistake. Students can see where corrections are required, and the color code system keeps you informed about the kinds of remedial help the kids may

Class Checklist

A checklist of things to consider when self editing a piece of writing will help pupils evaluate their creations. You might create a list of items you consider important, but a class created list of things to watch for will make it more important and personal.

Spend a few minutes each day for a week to create the list. The first day discuss writing content — the importance of a good idea, topic sentences, main idea, good supporting details, no unnecessary facts or unrelated ideas. Write one or more rules to cover these points.

The second day, discuss the importance of using interesting and colorful language, as well as correct spelling. Create rules about them. The third day take up punctuation; the fourth, grammar. On Friday, combine all the rules, reread them together, make any changes, then duplicate the lists so all pupils have a copy to refer to. Because it is their list, they will be more concerned with following its ideas.

Math

Introduction

The most complete math textbook series may still not include every technique you need to aid those pupils who are not sure about a particular process. The ideas in this chapter will supply those extra tips for reinforcing estimation skills, understanding fractional parts, and adding life to problem-solving techniques. They can be used as written or adapted to fit your special situation.

Ordering Activity

Print letters or numerals with a permanent marker on white plastic spoons. Mix up the spoons and stand them in a plastic foam base. Ask students to place them in order.

JUDY KEEPORTS

How Many Is 100?

Primary pupils often have difficulty conceptualizing large numbers. To make it easier, prepare a bulletin board with the caption "How Many Is 100?" Fill it with 100 paper objects arranged in ten rows of 10. Have students help cut out, color, and count 100 hearts in February, 100 shamrocks in March, 100 baseballs or spring flowers in April, and so on.

ELIZABETH TEICHER

Number Journal

Here's an idea that'll give plenty of practice writing numerals. Ask students to keep a number-writing journal. On each page, each student writes important numerals — phone numbers, addresses, birthdays, height or weight, number of family members, batting average of favorite baseball player, price of a bicycle. For each entry, the child writes a sentence telling the significance of the numeral.

PAULA GOINES

Number Concepts

Momma Kangaroo

Make a large kangaroo out of poster board and include the slit in her pouch. Also, make 10 baby kangaroos that will fit in the pouch and number them 1 through 10.

Pass the babies out to 10 students and tell them: "Momma kangaroo wants to take her babies to the park. She has so many babies she must count them to make sure she has not forgotten anyone." Have children count aloud as they put the babies in the pouch.

Or you can say, "Momma kangaroo has 10 babies. She could not decide upon names, so she numbered them. Now Momma needs help. Her babies are hiding and she needs to go home to cook dinner."

Pretend the kangaroo is calling her children. Have each child put the babies in the pouch as they are called.

DAWNA S. GANZ

Number Squares

Learning disabled children can enjoy success in counting, adding, subtracting, multiplying, and dividing by manipulating numbered squares and colored symbols.

Start with ten 9-by-12 inch sheets of oaktag. Divide each sheet into one-inch squares. On one sheet, write a zero on each square. On a second sheet, write the numeral 1 on each square, and so on through 9. On the reverse side of each square, use dots to illustrate the number value. Laminate for durability, then cut the squares apart. Cut out mathematical symbols—plus, minus, multiply, divide, equal sign—from stiff, colored paper.

Kids use the number squares and symbols to create and solve number problems. You can check answers with just a look.

DIANE MOON

Reading Inequality Signs

Elementary students will sometimes have difficulty reading a mathematical statement with an inequality symbol. Increase the readability of mathematical statements by telling students to spell the word "less" using the symbol < as a replacement for the letter "s" in the word. This mnemonic device helps students keep the symbols straight and decreases confusion.

GREGORY POROD

Math Bulletin Board

Divide a bulletin board into three sections and label them one, two, and three. Ask pupils to think of words to fit each section, such as solo, single, duo, duet, duplicate, double, triangle, trio, triple, and so on. Print the words under their proper headings. Encourage students to add other words to the display.

ISABEL LIVINGSTONE

Addition and Subtraction

All Aboard The Math Train!

For practice in addition and subtraction skills, have students line up to form a "train" around the classroom. Begin by dictating a problem to the first child in line. That child must answer correctly, then think of another problem where the first number is the same as the answer he or she has just given. The second child answers that problem, then thinks of one for the next person in line, and so on. You can keep score by giving students "tickets" and then punching holes in them every time they answer a problem correctly. When a child gives an incorrect answer, he or she does not receive a hole punch and must move to the end of the line to become the "caboose." In this way, no child has to sit out, and the whole class can participate for the entire "trip."

CHERYL MCLAUGHLIN

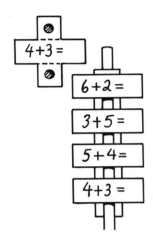

Magic Math Sticks

Use these easy, self-checking math sticks. Cut 3-inch squares from brightly colored construction paper. Next, cut a 1-inch square from each corner to form the "cross" figure shown in the illustration. Punch a hole in both the top and bottom ends of the cross and bend back. Write a math problem across the front and put the answer on the reverse side. Stack four or five on the straw by inserting it through the punched holes.

Children choose a stick and write the answers to each problem vertically on their paper. Twirl stick to check.

MARION WALKER

Top Hat Math

Children practice math facts playing this seasonal game. To make the game board, divide a large piece of poster board in half and draw an equal number of snowmen on each half. Write an addition sentence on each snowman. Cut out a hat for each, writing the answer to the problem on it. Kids sit at opposite ends and race to place the correct hats on their snowmen.

JUDY KEEPORTS

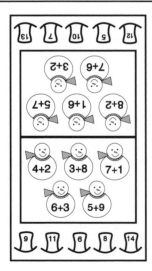

Using Concrete Objects

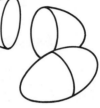

Egg-Citing Math

Colorful plastic eggs, available each spring, are inexpensive to buy. Use them to stimulate interest in learning and practicing math skills. Start with the activities on these two pages for primary and special education pupils, then create your own.

JEANE JOYNER AND MIRIAM LEIVA

Counting Activities

To demonstrate one-to-one correspondence, pass out a random number of eggs and a random number of cut-paper chickens. Ask children whether they have one chicken for each egg. Are there more chickens or more eggs? How do they know?

This activity can be extended to reinforce the concept of "how many more" when students explore comparison situations in preparation for subtraction problems. If there are eight children at a table and a basket of eggs, are there enough eggs in the basket for each child? How many more are needed?

Adding and Subtracting

Numeration activities might begin by having students group eggs into sets, matching a set to a card with pictures of eggs or a card with dots, and finally making sets matching numeral cards, and vice versa. For example, ask students to make a group with five eggs. It may require using all eggs in the basket to make sets of five. What could be said about each group? How many eggs would be in each group if the teacher added one egg? How many if the teacher took one egg away from the sets? These experiences are crucial to conservation of numbers and serve as readiness for addition and subtraction.

Young children may sort eggs by color and count them. How many eggs in the basket are pink? Yellow? If you put the purple and yellow eggs together, how many would it be? These questions should be discussed and recorded by the teacher and eventually by the students to reinforce bridging from the concrete to the abstract. Students should be able to express orally and write number sentences about combining sets of different colored eggs.

Alternate Counting Strategies

Would the number of eggs be the same if the students used other counting methods? Many children are not certain the answer will remain the same. Determining "how many eggs" gives the teacher opportunities to model alternate counting strategies. The situation is appropriate for teaching tallying. In tallying, students record a one-to-one correspondence between the eggs and marks they record on paper. Counting by fives and counting-on become part of the lesson.

Column Addition

Another method of determining how many would be to sort groups by color, count each set, and add groups together. Column addition is illustrated as students classify, count, record and explain the combining of sets.

Next, try arranging the eggs into groups of tens and ones to focus on place value. Have children remove ten eggs from the basket and keep them on their desks until all eggs are placed in groups of ten with "loose ones" left in the basket. Students who have ten eggs are instructed to stand, name the number of tens and then count by ones the number of eggs in the basket to find the total. Bridge to the abstract by writing on the board. For example, 3 tens and 5 ones are 35.

Estimating Numbers

The process of estimating requires teacher direction as children proceed through the steps: guess, guesstimate, estimate. To illustrate that estimates are answers arising from knowledge or experience, the teacher should bring the eggs to the class the next day in the same container. Tell students some of the eggs were removed. Ask them to visualize how many there were yesterday to move from guessing to estimating. Allow students to choose ways to count the eggs and verify estimates.

The teacher might use more eggs in the next exercise. By using the same container and items to be estimated, children can build on experience. They can relate "more" and "less" to the number of eggs handled previously. The focus is on giving a reasonable approximation, not the exact number of eggs.

Using Concrete Objects

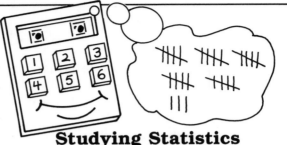

Learning To Graph

Graph the class's favorite colored eggs. This provides opportunities for students to collect, organize and display information. Pass a basket around, allowing each child to choose his or her favorite color egg. Have students group themselves by egg colors and decide how to label the graphing mat on which they will place their eggs. The teacher might ask students to explain what the graph means. Which color egg was the favorite? Was at least one of each color chosen? Which was the least popular color? Did more children choose blue or pink eggs? How many children participated? Do you think the graph would look the same in another class?

Students can also create a pictorial graph. Have each child glue a paper egg on a large graph to indicate his or her favorite color. Repeat questions previously asked to teach how to interpret graphs. Make a bar graph with the same information to carry the activity from concrete experience to an abstract record of the students' choices. JEANE JOYNER MIRIAM LEIVA

Studying Statistics

It is interesting to see if the same color would be chosen in the class next door. This is an interesting problem-solving situation which students can resolve based on their previous experience. Ask how students might find out about other students' preferences, and help them make a plan to collect the information. After students gather the data, have them make tallies and bar graphs to display results. Use calculators to combine survey results to help youngsters deal with numbers beyond their computational skills.

Students might also create symbol graphs, with one egg representing ten student choices. Students have little difficulty interpreting information on graphs they create when they have managed the project from start to finish.

JEANE JOYNER MIRIAM LEIVA

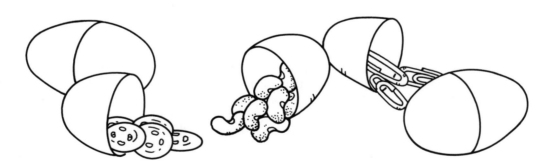

Volume and Other Concepts

Place different numbers, small objects or dried beans inside several eggs. Which egg contains the most? Explain. Count the objects in each egg. Continue to explore volume by comparing several different sizes of eggs filled with objects.

For multiplication, choose four eggs and place two beans in each. How many beans are in all? Record the arithmetic sentence and solution pictorially and numerically to bridge from concrete to abstract. For division, divide the beans equally among three students. How many beans does each person get? Are any left over?

JEANE JOYNER MIRIAM LEIVA

Four Math Operations

Triangular Flashcards

Divide your work while multiplying your effectiveness with this teaching aid. Cut equilateral triangles from tagboard. Write number facts on the cards with numbers in the corners as shown. When quizzing a student, hold the card by a corner, covering one number with your fingers. Make one set for addition/subtraction facts, another for multiplication/division. Each combination reinforces the relationship between the two operations. These self-checking cards are useful for independent work or practice at home with parents.

KATHY KLEIN

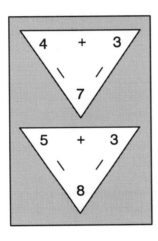

Same As

Use this card game to help kids practice basic facts for addition, subtraction, multiplication, and division. First, make a deck of playing cards with a variety of math problems—3x4, 6+6, 27÷3, 15-6. Be sure that for each problem, there is at least one other card with a different problem that has the same answer. Write only the problems, not the answers. To play, each child takes a turn drawing a card from the top of the deck and placing it face up on the table. As play continues, a row of cards will form on the table. The first student to identify two cards having the same answer calls "same as," keeps those cards, and is awarded the number of points they total. When all pairs have been identified, the game ends.

ANN MURRAY

Roll The Dice

To strengthen math skills, create practice problems using rolls of a die. Add, subtract, multiply and divide the numbers rolled. Two or three dice placed side by side create multidigit numbers.

Use one die, rolled multiple times, to make a point about places. A hundred thousand equals six places. Roll the die six times. Children determine how many rolls they need for hundreds, thousands, millions.

Pick a volunteer to record numbers as they are rolled. Students read the numbers and master places. Or, they can read the number as each place value is added and build on their success.

VITA MONASTERO

Speedster Math Drills

Develop speedy response to math problems and have fun doing it. Use five minutes every day to practice, reinforce or present new math facts. These drills build confidence while building speed.

Distribute basic fact sheets and let students know you will use the facts in oral problems. Fire off multiple-step problems such as:

$6 \times 2 + 8 \div 5 - 2 \times 9 + 3 \div 7.$

Use this level for beginners. Problems grow increasingly complex and the time between steps shortens as skills improve. More advanced problems might sound like this:

$4 \times 3 \times 10 - 20 \div 10 \times 5 - 40 \div 2.$

Work your way up to squares and cubes.

HENRY PAOLISSI

Multiplication

Multiply Interest For Math

When students are required to learn multiplication tables, they groan, thinking they are responsible for memorizing 100 facts. But this is not the case.

Since zero times any number equals zero, you can eliminate 20 facts to learn. And 2 x 1 = 2, so it does not need to be included in the twos, and so on. You get the same answer for 3 x 2 as 2 x 3, so delete one or the other all the way up on the basic multiplication chart. This eliminates 64 facts and leaves only 36 to learn — much more manageable from the student's point of view. You don't have to explain the basis for the deletions. Just present the multiplication chart to your students and cross out the 64 already-known or repetitive facts.

As a follow-up activity, prepare worksheets based on the basic chart and include a variety of patterns for students to find. Try to make each worksheet a little more difficult than the previous one.

As lessons begin on division, give students a short introduction to division, emphasizing that it is a reciprocal or opposite process to multiplication. Then, place the 36-fact chart on the board and fill in the twos yourself. Call on volunteers to fill in the rest of the chart. As the first worksheet, erase the answers and let children complete the chart. Continue with progressively difficult worksheets.

Based on worksheet scores, you'll find that students realize there are only 36 multiplication facts and 36 division facts to learn, and that multiplication and division are reciprocal processes, or, as they would say, that division is the opposite of multiplication.

HAROLD R. GERRY

Rap It Up!

I've noticed that many of my students are mesmerized by rap music. They spend hours listening to, memorizing, and reciting the lyrics to various rap songs. I decided to take advantage of their zeal and apply it to learning multiplication facts. I wrote this rap about the twelves table, and my students had it memorized in no time! Try it in your class, then enlist students' help in making others.

"Rap Twelve"
To learn your twelves can be a snap,
If we learn them by speaking Rap.
Twelve times two is twenty-four.
Say it now. You'll learn much more.
Twelve times three is thirty-six.
We tell no lies, we play no tricks.
Twelve times four is forty-eight.

Just the facts, Man, laid on straight.
Twelve times five is sixty, please.
You learn so fast, I'm weak in the knees.
Twelve times six, that's seventy-two.
Now, you know I wouldn't fool you!
Twelve times seven is eighty-four.
Wow! We're Cooking. Let's do some more.
Twelve times eight is ninety-six.
Totally rad! That's quite a mix.
Twelve times nine is one hundred eight.
Awesome, Man you're doing great!
Twelve times ten? That's one hundred twenty.
Two more to go and that will be plenty.
Twelve times eleven is one thirty-two.
You're learning fast. I'm proud of you!
Twelve times twelve is one forty-four.
You know them all. You know the score.

PAT GARWICH

Quick Math Drill

A "multiplication fish bowl" is a good way to review math facts. Place small cards with one-digit numbers written on them into a glass fishbowl. (Make sure the opening is large enough to easily slip a hand through.) To play, a pupil simply reaches in and picks any two cards. He or she looks at the two numbers, multiplies them, and then announces the product. This activity can also be used for number recognition, addition, or subtraction. It's perfect for those last few minutes before the bell rings.

GRETCHEN NEILSON

Estimating/Averages

Leaves, Leaves, Leaves

How many leaves are on a tree? Here's a fun estimation activity to incorporate into a math unit on leaves.

First, take students on a mini field trip around the school grounds or to a local park and ask them to count the leaves on one branch of a tree. Next, have kids figure out the average number of leaves per branch. Then count or estimate the number of branches on the tree to find the total number of leaves on the tree.

PAUL C. SPECTOR

More Or Less

Help students sharpen their estimation skills with this game. Have a student choose a number at random. Other students must guess what the number is. The student who chose the number signals them that the number is higher than the guess with a thumbs-up signal, or lower, with thumbs down. As students discover strategies for narrowing down the field of numbers, they should be able to guess the number in fewer tries. Have kids take turns being the leader. JOAN NOVELLI

Outdoor Math

Give kids a chance to test their measurement and estimation skills in this outdoor activity. On a sunny day, ask each child to choose an object — fence post, bush, playground swing — and measure the length of its shadow using yard or meter sticks or lengths of rope. Each records the measurement and time of day on a graph. Kids take additional measurements at lunch and once again before going home. If possible, give students several days to collect measurements. Then, on the next sunny day, send kids outside with measuring devices and ask them to use their data to estimate time of day — given the length of a shadow — or to estimate the shadow's length — given the time of day. Select several students to verify their estimates by measuring a shadow and reporting it to the class.

JEANNE ALDERSON

How Long Is A Minute?

Tell your students that you are giving them exactly one minute to think of all the things that would take them one minute to do. Next, ask them to write down each thing that they think they could do in a minute or less. Have students take turns reading what they have written. Other members of the class can agree or disagree about whether they think each activity would take just that many seconds. If the majority of the class disagrees, then ask several students to do the activity as homework, record the time it takes, and report the results of their experiments to the rest of the class the next day.

JANETTE CALLIS

Place Value/Decimals/Money

"Money" Makes Students Sit Up And Take Notice

Students seem to pay attention when money is involved. Here is a sure-fire incentive to make your math class interesting and fun. It is a banking system where you "print" your own money and reward students when they:

are on time; raise their hands; stay in their seats, answer questions correctly; turn in correct homework; and earn all A's.

Teachers should set fees, such as $10 for being on time and $5 for each time hands are raised.

Children owe you money when they do the following:

are tardy; eat or chew gum or candy; turn in incomplete assignments; use bad language; do not finish homework; talk out of turn; fight; and visit the office for disciplinary reasons.

Teachers set fees here also. Students may

have to come up with $20 for incomplete assignments, $150 for fighting and $5 for talking out of turn.

Establish banking days, such as Tuesdays and Thursdays. After a few weeks, students who have built up sizable accounts are eligible to buy privileges like time out, extra recess, a free class period, choice of seat, or they can add one point to their grade averages.

It's helpful to select a mayor, along with an assistant mayor, secretary, banker, security guards, and sanitation workers to help monitor the system.

WILLIAM BAYMNER

Place Acting

Help students get a clear picture of place value by acting out numbers. You decide how many places the number must have and the student makes up a number to portray. Determine in advance that stomping, for example, will represent hundreds, clapping denotes tens and ringing a bell means one. Classmates count the actions, record the count for each digit and figure out the number. JUDY VAN ACKER

Department Store Decimals

Department store sales flyers provide all you need for decimal fun. Pick up enough for everyone in your class. Write specific descriptions of eight to a dozen articles and send your students on a deskbound shopping trip through the flyers. Have them record both the original and sales price. Calculate the total cost each way and the difference.

DIANE STOLL

Percent Pun Fun

Reinforce math lessons and stimulate creative thinking with math "puns." After several lessons on percents, for example, put this question to the students: "What do you call someone who practices multiplication tables while jogging?" Provide students with these letter clues:

T: 6 is 25 percent of _____
M: 12.5 percent of 320 is _____
L: 20 is _____ percent of 80
H: 4 is 20 percent of _____
E: 25 percent of 140 is _____
A: _____ percent of 10 is 3

Now, to answer the riddle, put the letters in the spaces above the corresponding numerical answers:

__ __ __ __ __ __ __ __ __
30 40 30 24 20 25 35 24 35

Challenge kids to create their own puns. They can use riddle books for pun ideas, then develop their own math problems, codes and answer keys. Suggest that children exchange puzzles with their classmates. CAROL FRY

Economic Concepts

A Math Lesson Students Can Take To The Bank

Starting a class bank makes good "cents" when studying money. Class banking allows students to earn salaries, save, spend and invest. In the process, they learn about the ways money is used in "the real world."

Assigning jobs • In order for students to be able to earn money, they have to have a job. Think of jobs they can do in the classroom and assign "salaries" to them. For example, students can pick up litter from the school grounds or clean the class pet's cage.

Print each job, a description of the job to be done and the weekly salary on an index card. Laminate the cards for durability. Pass out the job description cards randomly.

Students complete the job and report to you. If the work has been done properly, the student gets credit for having done the work, and receives the salary. Use play money for currency or make your own.

Bank jobs • Students work for the bank in addition to their salaried jobs, with no additional pay.

Bank positions include bank president, vice president and teller. Responsibilities for the president and vice president include passing out salaries, opening and closing the bank and overseeing business. The tellers handle individual transactions with the students.

Rotating jobs • Rotate students' jobs (both salaried and nonsalaried) weekly so everyone gets a chance to try different jobs. Instead of training each student on a job after every job change, have the student leaving the position train the next person. This saves your time and gives students valuable experience in working together and giving directions.

Banking • Discuss budgeting and planning before beginning banking. The bank president distributes salaries on Friday so students can get advice over the weekend about banking plans. Banking Day is Monday.

Start out simply with deposits and withdrawals in checking and savings accounts. Give each student an empty bank book (which may be obtained from the local bank or made), a record sheet for transactions and a record card for bank personnel's use to record the students' names and balance records. Distribute deposit and withdrawal slips as needed.

Tellers mark new deposits or withdrawals on the record card, then initial and date the transactions on the card, the record sheet and the students' bank books.

If students wish to open checking accounts, they receive two bank books and the bank keeps two record cards — one for savings and the other for checking. They also receive checks.

Once a week, the bank president can send out statements on individual accounts, detailing transactions made during the month and the current balance.

Later, you may wish to introduce a lesson on interest and have students earn a set interest rate on their savings balances. Interest can also be included in the weekly bank statement.

Divide the class into two teams on banking day. One team banks while the other serves as bank personnel. Switch teams halfway through the time period. This gives everybody a chance to do both.

Make the room look like a bank by pushing desks against the walls for teller stands. Or, you may wish to make teller stalls from large cardboard boxes or wood.

Purchases • Not all of the students' money is deposited. There has to be something to purchase to make the lesson more realistic and fun. Ask students to brainstorm things worth buying in the classroom and make a list. From students' lists, make up cards representing products and services to be bought. When students buy the cards, write their names on a master list to keep track of who has what. A student vendor keeps track on a calendar of the dates the cards are returned.

Some cards can be used only once, others can be used all week. Once a card is used, it must be returned to the vendor. Fines can be assessed if cards are returned late. Purchases are made on Wednesday, so students are encouraged to budget and plan ahead.

Some items that can be sold are: use of the class soccer ball, free reading at the library, old books and dated lost and found items, adoption of the class pet during any holiday with a note from home, etc.

Offer several cards under the different categories such as sports, free activities, academic excellence, etc. This way there is something for every interest and ability level.

ELLEN WEBER

Banking Tools

Reproduce the banking forms below. Distribute several to each student to use on banking day.

NAME _____   DATE _____ 19 _____

CLASS _____

SCHOOL _____

PAY TO THE ORDER OF _____   AMOUNT _____
                                                  (NUMERALS)

AMOUNT _____
(WRITTEN)

SIGNATURE _____

SCHOOL
BANK

MEMO _____

DEPOSIT SLIP

NAME _____   ☐ CHECKING

CLASS _____

DATE _____   ☐ SAVINGS

SIGNATURE _____

AMT. OF CHECK _____

AMT. OF CASH _____

AMT. RECEIVED _____

TOTAL DEPOSIT _____

WITHDRAWAL SLIP

NAME _____   ☐ CHECKING

CLASS _____

DATE _____   ☐ SAVINGS

SIGNATURE _____

AMT. FROM CHECKING _____

AMT. FROM SAVINGS _____

NEW TOTAL CHECKING _____

NEW TOTAL SAVINGS _____

Fractions

Fraction Action

Fraction cubes and strips enhance fraction activities. Cubes are commercially available, but you can make your own with dice. Cut blank gummed labels the same size as the faces of a die. Cover the dots, then label sides 1/2, 1/4, 1/6, 1/8, and 1/16 (leave the sixth side blank or repeat a fraction).

Make fraction strips from 9-by-12-inch sheets of red, blue, yellow, green, orange, and purple construction paper. Cut into 2-inch-wide strips. Leave the red strips intact at 12 inches. Cut the blue strips in half; cut the yellow in fourths, the green in sixths, the orange in eighths, and the purple in sixteenths. Label the strips with the appropriate fractions and laminate. If children are making individual sets, each should have one red, two blue, four yellow, six green, eight orange, and 16 purple strips.

With these sets, kids can play two variations on a fraction game.

Cover Up

Use as a quick review. Each player begins with a red (whole) strip. Players take turns rolling the cube. The fraction face up indicates the size piece the player draws, from a pile or from the child's own set, to place on the red strip. A player must roll a fraction combination that exactly equals one to win.

Uncover

Review equivalent fractions with this version. Each player begins with a red (whole) strip covered with two blue (1/2) strips. Players take turns rolling the cube. The fraction face up is the amount they can remove from the strip. For example, if a player rolls 1/4, he or she places one blue 1/2 strip in the discard pile and picks up a yellow 1/4 strip to place on the red strip. To completely uncover the red strip, a player must roll a fraction smaller than or equal to fractions remaining on the red — larger fractions don't count. The first to uncover the strip wins.

Adding

If each child has a set of fraction strips, use them in whole-group sessions. You might ask kids to create a fraction equation that equals one. Ask a volunteer to write an example on the chalkboard:

$$1/4+1/4+1/4+1/8+1/8=1$$

Review addition of fractions by writing this equation under the first:

$$3/4+2/8=1$$

Ask kids to compare two 1/8 pieces with one 1/4 strip to demonstrate how 2/8 can be reduced to its lowest terms and still equal the same size.

Greater Than, Less Than

You can also use the strips to demonstrate greater than and less than and to practice operations, like subtraction and division. Encourage children to make up their own games with the strips. Start the fraction action in your classroom—it won't stop!

JOHN JAMES

Fraction Collage

You'll need large pieces of tagboard, old magazines, and glue. Give kids large pieces of tagboard and then have them cut out pictures from the magazines that represent their favorite things, ambitions, hobbies, and so on. Have kids glue the pictures to the tagboard, without overlapping the pictures. Next, have each child count the number of pictures used to make his or her collage and use that number as a denominator. Have students compute what fractions of their collages contain specific pictures, such as animals, flowers, sports, food, cars, and so on. If a student's collage has 15 pictures of animals, the fraction represented is 15/30, or one half of the pictures feature animals. Encourage kids to share their fraction collages with each other, then post them on the bulletin board or arrange them in a lively display.

KATHY FAGGELLA

Graphing

Graph Bulletin Board

Draw a grid on a large piece of poster board or paper and display on a bulletin board. The dimensions will depend on the size of the board. Mount a picture of each child in the class on an index card and laminate it. Trim each card to fit inside the boxes on the grid.

Display a question above the graph, such as "What method of transportation do you use to get to school?" Questions can be asked about current events, holidays, self, your particular curriculum, etc.

Put an index card with a category written on it at the bottom of the graph in each grid. For example, cars could be labeled "bus, walking, bike, car," etc.

The students post their pictures in the appropriate column.

When the graph is completed, use it as a basis for math questions, such as "How many students in this class ride the bus?" "Do more students walk than ride?," etc.

Not only do students have a visual point to refer to when working on math questions, but they also learn about bar graphs and how to make them.   ALEXA PERLMUTTER

What Method of transportation do you take to school?				
Bus	☻	☻	☻	☻
Walk	☻	☻	☻	
Bike	☻	☻		
Car	☻	☻	☻	
Other	☻	☻		

Toothpick Hunt

While the weather is still warm, try a toothpick hunt! This is a chance to combine a lesson in camouflage and graphing. Start with 100 toothpicks each of red, blue, yellow and green, or halved art sticks. Tape a sample of each color on the board.

Ask students to estimate how many of each color they will be able to find once they are scattered on the school lawn. Have them predict which colors will be found in order from most to least and explain the reasons for their predictions.

Find an area large enough so students can search one part of the playground. Provide small bags for the toothpicks.

After the hunt, have the class sort out and count toothpicks.

Discuss the results. Which toothpicks were the hardest to find? Easiest? Make a graph on the board to compare the students' predictions with the outcome.

Introduce or reinforce concepts of camouflage. Talk about protective coloration of plants and animals. Also introduce the idea that some colors can be seen more readily than others. Talk about the purpose of brightly colored emergency vehicles. Do follow-up experiments with color cards to see which colors can be seen from the greatest distances. Record results on a graph.   MYRA FEENEY

Great Graph!

To reinforce graphing skills, have children take a schoolwide survey of their classmates' and teachers' favorite musical performers. Students create the survey forms and distribute them throughout the school. After the forms have been returned, students compile the information in a bar graph on the bulletin board, indicating classmates' preferences in black, teachers' in red. To give the graph some showbiz style, have the children bring in pictures of their favorite performers and attach them to the bulletin board. The choices in my school ranged from Frank Sinatra to the Fat Boys!   MARC SOCOL

Metrics

Metric Scavenger Hunt

To give kids a fun lesson in applying metric measurements, try this new twist on an old favorite.

After children are familiar with using the metric system of measurement, let them go on a scavenger hunt around the school. Divide the class into groups and make a list of things to find, such as an item 1 meter long, an item 1 centimeter long, an item that holds 1 liter of water, and so on. Let kids approximate the items' measurements on the hunt, and then get accurate measurements when they return to the classroom. The group that comes closest to the specified measurements is the winner.   NAN SWEENEY

What Does It Weigh?

On a table or other flat surface, place various objects, such as paper clips, a pocket mirror, set of keys, tape dispenser and several pencils. Have students estimate the weight of each in metric measures. Then, have students check the estimates by actually weighing each item.
MARLOW EDIGER

How Far Away?

To reinforce the concept of metric measurement, place a dowel rod securely upright on the floor. Students then throw rings to "ring" the dowel rod. Each attempt is measured by students using metric linear measures.   MARLOW EDIGER

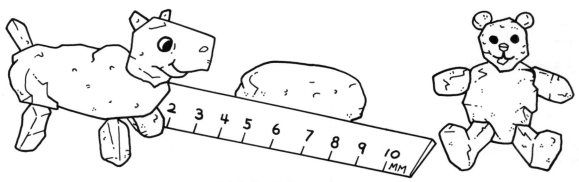

Metric Monsters

Here's a nature art project that integrates metric measurement. To create stone beasts, kids collect an assortment of pebbles—fist size or smaller—that suggest animal body parts such as eyes, ears, noses, tails, and beaks. Flat circular stones can become an animal's head, body, or leg.

Students experiment with the stones, trying different possibilities for heads, bodies, features, and appendages. When they have a working model, children label the parts of their creature for easy reference — RFL for right front leg, H for head, T for tail.

Before assembling the stone figure, each child measures the body parts to the nearest millimeter, recording the data on a fact sheet. Kids also record the weight of each stone in grams. Students can measure the volume of the stones by displacement of water — drop the stone in a beaker of water, then measure the increased water level in milliliters.

When measuring is completed, kids use white glue to seal parts together. Keep stones in place while glue sets by pressing a band of clay around each figure. Leave the metric monsters in their natural state or paint with tempera. Kids provide details — spots, stripes, eyelashes — using felt-tipped, permanent markers.

Display the beasts with record sheets to create a class menagerie.   BRIAN HEINZ

Measurement

So Big

Imagining a dinosaur's length is difficult for young children. Illustrate its huge size by having students "earn" the length of a dinosaur, foot by foot.

First, select a dinosaur, such as Stegosaurus or Tyrannosaurus Rex, and announce the number of feet the class will need to earn. Have on hand strong tape and foot-long strips of sturdy paper to equal the dinosaur's length. Then explain how they'll do it: For each dinosaur activity a student completes, he or she tapes one strip to a cumulative class roll.

Designate a variety of all-group and independent activities to complete for credit. For example, ask kids to memorize spelling words pertaining to dinosaurs or work math problems featuring dinosaur statistics. Introduce new vocabulary words beginning with each letter in the name of a particular dinosaur. Ask students to practice handwriting on dinosaur footprint stationery, then write a message to their favorite lizard!

When the length of the dinosaur has been earned, take the children outdoors or to a long hall. Space them so they can hold the strip taut as you unroll it. They're sure to appreciate, and be amazed at, just how long their dinosaur was! SANDRA J. FREY

Durable, Plastic Tanagrams

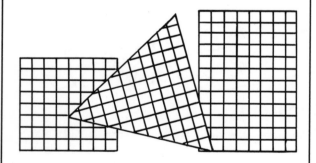

Save time, money and energy with this new slant on tanagram pieces! Tanagrams are geometric puzzles made by combining simple geometric shapes to form more complex ones. The puzzle cards, made of cardboard, contain the traced outline of the combined puzzle pieces. What's new? Plastic needlepoint mesh, which is ideal for making the geometric-shaped pieces! The material is durable, accurate and washable. Simply count the squares to cut perfect pieces. Laminate the puzzle cards to make them durable, too. MARILYN SMITH

Gallon Friend

"Gallon Friend" can be used on a bulletin board display to teach children the equations for pints, quarts and gallons. Individual Gallon Friends can be made for students' personal use as well. Cut a circle for the body from colorful construction paper. Cut arms and legs from a different colored piece of construction paper. Cut feet and hands from a third color of construction paper. Label the body "gallon," the legs and arms "quart" and the hands and feet "pint." Cut a circle for Gallon Friend's head and add hair, eyes, nose and mouth. Students can see by looking at Gallon Friend that two pints equal a quart, eight pints equal a gallon and four quarts equal a gallon.
SYLVIA LASSMAN

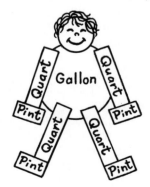

Word Problems

Personalized Math Problems

Want to get kids excited about word problems? Get personal! Photocopy a page of word problems from your math workbook, then cover any names found in the problems; photocopy again. This version will serve as a master copy. All you need to do is fill in the names of children in your class and make as many copies as you need. Kids will be delighted to read word problems about themselves.
RAY DILLON

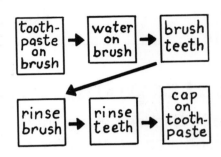

Follow The Flow Chart

Encourage students to approach math problems in a logical, step-by-step way by conducting a lesson on flow charts. Begin by having students choose a simple activity to break down into steps for a flow chart. Good examples include tying a shoelace, unwrapping and eating a piece of candy, brushing your teeth, and so on. Students then write down each step involved in the chosen activity inside a box, with an arrow pointing from it to the box containing the next step. The result? Clear, progressive thinking when attacking math problems.   KEN BIERLY

Story Problems

Ask students to role-play activities that require math, such as shopping, cooking, or building. At the end of each scene, kids write problems that correspond with their story.
DOROTHY ZJAWIN

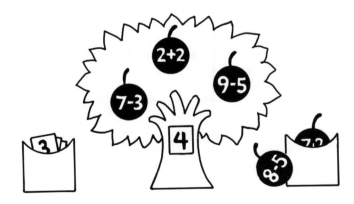

Mathematical Tree

Cut out at least 10 cherries and print a math problem on each, choosing mostly problems that have the same answer. Leave the answers off the cherries. Place the main answer numeral on the trunk of the tree. Kids examine the cherries and "hang" only those with problems that match the answer on the trunk. Variations: Ask children to create their own problems for others to solve. Vary the math operations, and gradually increase the difficulty of the problems.
BRENDA VANNESS

Word Problems

Caterpillar Pies

Ickee N. Slickee has invented a new fast-food craze, Caterpillar pies. He uses caterpillars of different colors and sizes to spice up his pies and give them a distinctive taste. Help him solve these problems so he can bake more pies.

1. Ickee sold 3 1/2 Hairy Berry pies and 4 1/8 Wormy Apple pies. What is the total?

_____

2. Each Fruit and Fly pie costs $6.75. How much did it cost your sister to buy 10 Fruit and Fly pies?

_____

3. Your principal treated all of the teachers to Chocolate Caterpillar pie. The bill came to $18.58. How much change did he get from a $20 bill?

_____

4. Ickee uses 3/4 of a cup of sugar for each pie. How much sugar does it take for 12 pies?

_____

5. Your best friend bought nine Bug and Berry pies. He gave you 3 1/4 of the pies. How many does he have left?

_____

6. Ickee uses 30 caterpillars for the crust of each of his Crusty Caterpillar Delights. How many crusts can he make with 960 caterpillars?

_____

7. Your mother bought dinner at Ickee's. She spent $31.24 on Hairy Berry pies and $24.56 on Chocolate Caterpillar pies. How much did she spend in all?

_____

8. Ickee uses 40 super-sized caterpillars for each Bug and Berry pie. How many super-sized caterpillars will he need for 36 Bug and Berry pies?

_____

9. Ickee sold 11 Fruit and Fly pies to your teacher. Each pie cost $6.75. How much did your teacher spend for all 11 pies?

_____

10. Your friend gave Ickee a $10 bill for a pie which cost $4.79. How much change did your friend receive?

_____

11. Ickee uses 3 1/2 orange caterpillars in each Chocolate Caterpillar pie. How many orange caterpillars does he need for 20 pies?

_____

Answers:
1. 7 5/8 pies (addition)
2. $67.50 (multiplication)
3. $1.42 (subtraction)
4. 9 cups (multiplication)
5. 5 3/4 pies (subtraction)
6. 32 crusts (division)
7. $55.80 (addition)
8. 1,440 caterpillars (multiplication)
9. $74.25 (multiplication)
10. $5.21 (subtraction)
11. 70 orange caterpillars (multiplication)

Other Number Bases

Journey To Planet Seven

Use an imaginary journey to Planet Seven to introduce the concept of number systems not based on 10. Begin by unveiling a rocket and planet that will become the centerpiece for student work. To prepare for the voyage, review place value.

Have kids read large numbers to partners from cards. Begin with single-digit numbers, then add digits so students can see patterns: 3; 23; 423; 6,423; 56,423; 956,423.

Prepare place-value charts, with 1s, 10s, 100s, 1000s at the top, and ask kids to write large numbers as you dictate them. What does 234 mean? (Two groups of 100, three groups of 10, four 1s.)

Review how the value of a digit depends on its position: 281; 8,122.

Ask the kids to dissect numbers: $5,432 = 5,000 + 400 + 30 + 2 = (5 \times 1,000) + (4 \times 100) + (3 \times 10) + (2 \times 1) = (5 \times 10^3) + (4 \times 10^2) + (3 \times 10^1) + (2 \times 10^0)$.

Extraterrestrial Activities

Write numbers on the board such as 14_7 and 32_7, and have students arrange that number of chips or buttons according to base 7.

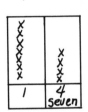
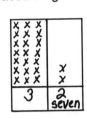

Give children single-digit addition and subtraction problems. As in base 10, kids will need to regroup numbers. Gradually include operations with two-digit numbers, then advance on to multiplication and division.

Let kids design bills or coins to be used as currency on Planet Seven. Ask them to draw imaginative pictures of Sevenites.

Leave Planet Seven and travel to other places, where your math team can develop base 5 and base 8. Then travel to a really far-out

a)	b)
4 seven	23 seven
+ 3 seven	+ 44 seven
10 seven	100 seven
c)	d)
10 seven	30 seven
− 2 seven	22 seven
5 seven	25 seven

planet where kids must develop a base 12 system. Let children make up their own symbols for the two new digits they'll need for this system (0, 1, 2, 3, 4, 5, 6, 7, 8, 9, *, #).

Galatic activities like these, besides being fun, will help your students learn how our number system works and understand the real meaning behind a digit's position in a number.

ELLEN GOW

Countdown And Launch

Point out that the base of our decimal system —10—is the number of fingers we have. Ask kids to count on their fingers while you record the numbers. Then ask: When we've counted them all, do we create another symbol as we did for 0-9? No, we combine 1 and 0 to create 10, representing one set of fingers and no singles left over.

Have the class count to 50 aloud. Proceed from 0 to 9 normally, then count: 1,0 (10); 1,1 (11); 1,2 (12); ...At 50, ask what will happen at 99. The next number is 100 and it means one group of 100, no 10s, no 1s.

Now tell students they're ready to take off. After some imaginary space travel, explain that once you land on Planet Seven, you will find that its inhabitants look different — they have seven fingers, five on one hand and two on the other. It's the team's job to help Sevenites develop a system of counting. Have kids hold up their hands with just the thumb and forefinger showing on one hand. What happens when Sevenites want to count higher than 6? To us the number 10 represents this number of objects: xxxxxxxxxx. To Sevenites the number 10 represents this amount: xxxxxxx. Continue to count with kids while filling in a base 7 chart (counting 1,1; 1,2; 1,3; and so on, as shown here).

Recycled Math

The Pricing Game

Save your Sunday newspaper and cut out car sale advertisements. Cut out construction paper in the shape of price tags. Duplicate photos of automobiles and glue onto the tags. Write the price of the cars in numeral form underneath their pictures. Make another set of tags to correspond with each picture tag, but with the prices written in word numerals. Ask students to match the words with the correct numerical notation.

CARLEEN MCCOY

Magazine Math

Here's an eye-catching bulletin board idea that integrates language arts and math. Have students cut out colorful pictures from magazines, then write a related math word problem on an index card. Next, kids attach the pictures to the cards and exchange cards with a partner to solve the math problems. Affix cards to the bulletin board for an interesting display. Not only must students use math skills, but they must also carefully proofread their work for errors in spelling, punctuation, and sentence structure.

MARY ANN BRENSEL

Math Fun Cards

Create practice math games from cutouts of old calendars. Supply calendars and 5x8 index cards. Students cut and paste numbers from calendars to assemble simple or complex math problems.

Students work out the answers on the back of each card. You check answers and file in the math corner. Make sure students include their names so you can target any students who miss their own problems. Students can create and solve problems in their free time.

VITA MONASTERO

Curriculum By The Calendar

Here are some suggestions for incorporating calendars into your curriculum. Let students find their own birthdates on calendars and color them.

Students can count how many classmates have birthdays in each month. Ask how many days are in a week, month. Discuss leap year.

A calendar can help solve math problems. Ask what day students would return from a two-week vacation, counting only business days.

Reading and spelling words can come from calendars, too.

And, pages can be glued to cardboard and cut apart to make jigsaw puzzles.

AILEEN MALLORY

Recycled Math

Can We Shop?

To reinforce skills in problem solving, decision making, and math, try this shopping spree activity. Begin by collecting colorful sales circulars from newspapers; one for each child in your class. Put different denominations of play money (up to several hundred dollars) in plain envelopes, one for each pupil. Then have kids use the play money to go on a shopping spree through the sale fliers. Children will need to count their monies, choose items from the flier, then subtract from the total. Students should try to spend all their money — excess amounts must be returned. Extend the activity by having kids use calculators to check one another's addition and subtraction.

KATHY FAGGELLA

Save Those Coupons

Don't throw away store coupons! They can be a valuable classroom learning tool.

Students can set up a bank, using coupons as money for making deposits, loans and change.

Provide students with grocery advertisements and coupons. Ask each student to make a shopping list and determine how much money he or she can save using coupons.

Coupons can also be used for achievement tokens; these can be redeemed for small gifts which are given a coupon value. JEAN STANGL

Magamath

Don't throw away those extra stamps used to advertise magazine subscriptions. Redeem them for a bargain math lesson.

Distribute a different stamp to each child in the class. Ask students to identify the following information about each magazine: its name, regular subscription price, single copy price, number of issues, and special subscription offer. Kids compare cost per issue for the regular subscription, single copy, and special offer to decide which is really the best bargain.

ROBERTA MAYERHOFF

Math Review

Ongoing Math Review

Keep students' math skills current by providing a daily and weekly quiz. Train students to do the review during transition time (such as after recess) to gain class time.

Each day have students solve at least three, but no more than five, review problems. The problems should include skills taught at the beginning of the school year to the present, but should not introduce a new skill. In a week, students should solve at least one problem for all important skills taught.

Limit the time for the activity to 5 or 10 minutes. Some students may not finish, but the key element of this technique is immediate oral discussion and self-grading. Talk through the solution to each problem (spending more time on skills that may not have been mastered by the entire class). Even students who have not completed the activity can do so as you solve the problems together.

You may wish to provide work sheets to go with the weekly review questions. Keep master copies for future use.

TAMARA S. SCOTT

Automath-It

Here's how to perk up math and identify concepts kids find difficult.

Draw and cut out your own version of a math machine, one large enough to tack up as a bulletin board display. As students work on math problems independently, they use scrap paper or index cards to write down any problems that they need help with. These they tack to the Math Machine bulletin board.

At the end of the day, check the board to determine the areas the class or individual students need help with. Or, let student Math Machine Assistants check the day's cases and see if they can solve the problems.

LINDA MERCER

Math Review

Stand Up

Call on a capable student to answer a problem, for example, 80 times 90. Call on another child, less sure of his or her math facts, for the reversal, 90 times 80.

Paying attention provides the correct answer. If a student was tuning into a private ball game instead of you and answers incorrectly, he or she must stand. The student remains standing until another child misses the reverse fact or until you ask him or her another problem.

These "stand-up, sit-downs" are a marvelous weapon against inattention.

ROBERT W. SMITH

Math Relay

Make a game out of math practice problems by turning this exercise into a relay. Write 3 columns of 4 problems each on the board. Divide students into 3 teams of 4 each. Have one student from each team work a problem. When finished, he or she passes a baton to the next person on the team. First team to complete all problems wins.

Empty paper towel rolls covered with paper or paint make ideal batons. DIANNE LEAHY

Number Jump

Here's a quick game that's great math "exercise." First, whisper a different multiplication product to each student. Kids keep their numbers secret until the game begins. Next, students form a circle and crouch so that knees are bent and hands touch the ground. Then you call out a multiplication problem. If it equals a student's secret number, he or she jumps up and calls out the answer. The child then returns to the crouch position and awaits another problem equal to his or her product.

You can adapt this for lower-grade students, who may know fewer products, by whispering the same number to several kids. They jump up at the same time. This game can also be used for addition, subtraction, and division.

BETH DIAZ

4 Social Studies

Introduction

What can I do to make historical events more exciting? How can I help pupils understand the lines on a map and be able to interpret them? If you have these kinds of questions, then you will want to read this chapter. Timelines of events will give pupils a sense of history they will remember. Through other ideas the community, state, country and the world all take on new dimensions.

Make A Map

By creating a map of the classroom together, you can help students begin to understand that a map is a "bird's eye view" of an area.

First, ask kids to imagine they can fly up to the ceiling and look down upon the classroom. Discuss how your room might look from that perspective (smaller, wider).

Now place a sheet of butcher paper on the floor, and ask kids to gather around it. Cut paper figures to represent key features in the room. Glue these onto the map where children agree they belong. Help kids with this task by asking them to think about how the classroom is arranged. What's next to the block corner? To the easels?

When the map is done, ask children for ideas of how you might use it.

MARGARET JOQUE WILLIAMS

Map Reading

Make cardboard window frames to help primary students develop map skills. When you place a frame on a large map, it encourages kids to focus on small areas for detail.

To make each frame, use a piece of cardboard 5 inches by 8 inches. Cut out the inside to leave a 3/4-inch border on all sides.

Mount a map on posterboard. Kids can attach the window frames with pushpins or just hold them in place. Ask students to take turns finding and framing a specific city, river, or other geographic feature.

PAM KRIEPS

Map Skills

Latitude And Longitude

To review the concepts of latitude and longitude, try this hands-on activity. Give each pupil the following items: a 9-inch paper plate, four blank index cards, three 10-inch pieces of yarn in red, blue, and orange, and a folder for storing the materials.

First have children draw lines representing degrees of longitude and latitude on their paper plates. Then ask them to write each of the four cardinal directions on the index cards, one direction per card. Have each pupil place the paper plate in the middle of his or her desk and surround it with the four directional cards, arranged in their correct positions (the top of the plate is north, the bottom is south, and so on). Tell the students that the plate represents earth. Next, have the students use red yarn to represent the equator, blue to show longitude, and orange for latitude. Ask pupils to demonstrate locations with the blue yarn, such as 20 degrees east longitude, 40 degrees west longitude, and so on. Then ask them to show 20 degrees north latitude and 40 degrees south latitude with the orange yarn. Finally, have them show a meridian with blue yarn and a parallel with orange yarn. Students can do this activity individually or with a partner.

LINDA HALAS

Teaching Longitude And Latitude

Try this simple activity to introduce the study of longitude and latitude. Give each child a sheet of plain white paper, then ask students to draw certain objects anywhere on their papers. Objects might include a red triangle, blue circle, green rectangle, two yellow squares, four purple stars, and eight squiggly lines.

Now call on a student and ask him or her to tell you where the red triangle is located on his or her paper. You should receive an answer like "near the top" or "towards the bottom." Try this a few times with different students and objects. Then point out how difficult it is to precisely indicate the locations of the objects.

Next, have students accordion-fold their papers vertically six or seven times, then unfold them and draw pencil lines over the creases. Have them repeat the process horizontally. Finally, have students label the vertical lines with letters and the horizontal lines with numbers.

Now have students give you more precise locations by calling out the letters and numbers of intersecting lines closest to the objects in question. This way, you'll have set the stage for a meaningful discussion of longitude and latitude.

FLORENCE RIVES

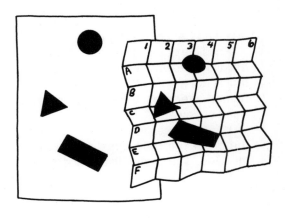

Our Community

County Classrooms

Illustrate social studies concepts about communities and how they function with real examples from your own county or community.

Begin with a class visit to the county courthouse or city hall. Prior to the trip, preview with the class the names of departments — sheriff, zoning board, assessor, health. Arrange to have a representative give a short explanation during the visit of the functions of various agencies.

Review map skills and explore geographic features with a map from the surveyor's office. Using your town or city as the center, draw a circle with a 15-mile radius. Then, ask students to list towns and villages or neighborhoods and public parks within the circle. Help kids locate places named for geographic features — River City, Mount Holly, High Falls — and to identify places named for famous people and events. Kids might also look for names revealing native American origins, or they might trace economic history in place names such as Milltown, Coalville, and Oil City.

Using the map, ask students to list ways people and goods travel within the area. Lists may include interstate highways, county roads, railroad tracks, airports, lakes, rivers, and canals. Then ask kids to consider methods of transportation that might be used in your area in the future.

Ask pupils to research county or city businesses and occupations using the local yellow pages and newspapers. Students list different businesses found in your area and record employment opportunities advertised in the newspaper's classified sections. Invite a member of the chamber of commerce to speak about local business goals for the future. Students might enjoy imagining new businesses and writing advertisements for products or services.

Finish your study with a Seniors-Juniors Day. Invite members of the local historical society or longtime residents to tell kids about the county's or city's past by sharing scrapbooks and photos. Students can share their vision of the area's future industry and transportation systems with their guests through drawings and writings.

WILLIAM CROWDER

Know-Your-Town Scavenger Hunt

Familiarize your class with your hometown by having a scavenger hunt. Organize students into teams of three or four. Give each group a list of questions about the town. The questions may be the same for each team, or you may want to give each team a few special questions. Discuss places to find the answers to the questions, such as a city map, the library, museum, etc.

Possible questions might include: What is the oldest building in town? What is the newest building in town that is not a home? How many streets or avenues are named after presidents? How many are named after trees or flowers?

Vary the questions to suit your community, tailoring the difficulty of the questions to the age of students involved. The team with the most correct answers is the winner.

KELLY RILEY

The States

Where Am I?

Play this variation of "Pin the Tail on the Donkey" to reinforce U.S. geography lessons.

Blindfold a child and give him or her a pushpin. Position the child in front of a map of the United States. Then he or she pushes the pin into the map and tries to guess which state the pin is in by asking questions, such as: "Am I west of the Mississippi?" "Do I border Canada?" "Do I border the Atlantic?" After five questions, the player must guess the state.

Both the player and class members who are answering the player's questions will strengthen their knowledge of U.S. geography.

ISOBEL LIVINGSTONE

Map Skills Builder

Build students' map skills by covering a bulletin board with the outline of the United States. Outline each of the 50 states. Have students compile a list of all the National Football League (NFL) teams. Students label all of the states and cities on the map that are home to NFL teams.

Print questions on pieces of construction paper regarding NFL teams and their states to help students master geography, such as "Which state has the most NFL teams?" or "Where do the Redskins play?" Laminate the questions. Attach a construction paper pocket to the board to hold questions.

SUE ROTH

50-State Review

Put some zip into your class review of the states with this activity.

Have each student select a state and create an appropriate license plate for it. Encourage kids to convey as much as possible about their states through a combination of illustrations, letters, and numbers.

Students may want to illustrate state flowers, state birds, shapes of the states, historical events, and man-made or natural landmarks. Encourage them to use their imaginations when devising license plate letters and numbers, too. For example, "ORIG-13" would be good to use for one of the original 13 states.

REBECCA WEBSTER GRAVES

The States

State Study

A batiked and embroidered quilt is a great way to culminate a study and review of your state. This 7-by 9-foot quilt of Iowa outlines each county's shape and highlights a notable attraction or activity taking place there. After students researched, designed, batiked and embroidered each county, a volunteer sewed the pieces together and applied the quilt backing. It won an award at the State Fair and was displayed at the state capitol.

Creating the quilt required students to use language, mathematics, decision-making, sequential learning and art and map skills.

SUE D. JENSEN   MARILYN CAVES

A Designer Original

A student-designed skirt is a finishing touch to a study of the 50 states. Here's how your class can make one: First, put the name of each state on a slip of paper. Every student selects a slip and draws the state's outline on a 5-by 7-inch piece of paper. Next, each child researches the state bird, tree, and flower and chooses one other interesting fact to include on the drawing. During sharing time, children explain their drawings, and post them around a large U.S. map on your bulletin board. Ask kids to also point out their state on the map so everyone gets a general picture of the location in relationship to your home state. Kids continue to draw and research states until all are completed.

As a culminating activity, mark a large piece of white muslin into 5-by 7-inch blocks. Provide permanent markers so kids can illustrate their states in the spaces. Don't tell your students that you are going to sew the material into a floor-length skirt. Just wear it to school!

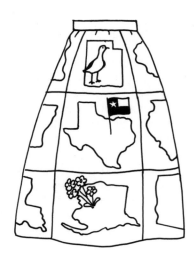

Try class designs based on lessons about anything, from the planets to the months of the year. The result will be learning treasures to save for years.

JANE E. KRUSE

"Palatable" Study Of The U.S.

Here's a fun activity to whet your students' appetite for geography! Obtain names of elementary or middle schools in other states from fellow teachers, magazines, news articles, the Yellow Pages, etc.

Have the class work together to compose a form letter to classes in other states explaining they are studying the U.S. and are writing to one class in each state to ask for their help. The letter should ask the classes they are corresponding with to write a few sentences describing their state and to enclose a favorite regional recipe. State a deadline for the material to be submitted.

To encourage uniformity in response, enclose a form with space to write in comments, class members' names, the address, city and state of the school, and a spot for the recipe.

Have your students copy the master letter, each addressing his or her letter to a different school in a different state. Have students direct the letters to the principal, teacher of a certain class (if known), or to a particular grade.

Repeat this activity until a letter has been sent to a school in each of the 50 states.

When the responses come in, reproduce, collate, and put them into book form. Distribute the books to class members.

Spend some time each day with the class locating the towns of the respondents. Assign volunteers to prepare and bring in some of the recipes submitted. Then have a tasting party to sample them.

You may hear from students living on islands, in desert areas, the Great Plains or a mountain valley, and you may receive some interesting recipes as well. Not only will students learn a bit about geography, but they will also learn a lesson in cultural geography.

As a thank-you to participants, offer to send a copy of the book.

SANDRA FREY

President Stamp Activity

Use this postage stamp activity to teach your students about the U.S. presidents and geography.

Obtain a set of stamps from the post office featuring U.S. presidents. Students then use maps to locate towns or cities named after presidents. Students make a list of these towns. When the list is complete, students look up the zip code of the city or town in a zip code book. Then, students write a letter to the postmaster of the town. Included with the letter is a self-addressed envelope stamped with the stamp of the president for whom the city or town was named. In the letter, students ask the postmaster to mail the self-addressed stamped envelope back to the class with the cancelled stamp.

The class will have a full set of cancelled presidential stamps postmarked in the towns named for them.

This makes a great geography and history lesson, and the letter-writing provides a language arts lesson.

SISTER JOANNE FRANCIS

The States

Name Mobiles

Here's a great way for students to organize and share information gleaned from social studies research. Ask individuals or research teams to spell out the name of a state or country using uniformly cut 9-by 12-inch letters. Students write facts about the place — climate, geography, famous people, products, cities — grouping a different set of facts on each letter. Kids may want to paste photographs and illustrations on letters, too. Punch holes at the top and bottom of each letter, then tie together with string or yarn. Tack to a wall.   JANET REUTER

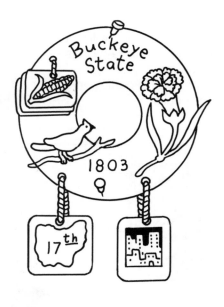

Where Is It?

Play the world or state geography game. Use a wall-size map. Divide the class into two teams. A player from each team goes to the map. You give the name of a city, state, country, river, etc. The first person to find it earns a point for his or her team.

Football Geography

Give each student an outline map of the United States. Then try out some of these map-skill activities.

Ask students to use atlases to locate a favorite football team's city on the map. Kids mark the city on the map using an appropriate symbol, such as a dot for a small city, a circle for a major city, or a star in a circle for a state capital.

Each week, students keep track of where their team is playing. In which directions is the team traveling and how many miles is it covering? What changes in topography might players see from their jet windows? Help children figure out how many time zones their team has crossed and what changes in climate it has experienced. Finally, ask students to imagine what it might be like to play a game in Mile High Stadium in Denver compared with playing one in Joe Robie Stadium in Miami.   DAVID APPLEBY

Where In The World?

This activity will help students become more familiar with the names and locations of cities and countries around the world. Begin by putting large maps of the United States and the world on your classroom walls or bulletin boards. When something important happens in the news, discuss the event with your students, then have them draw small pictures on index cards to illustrate it. When the drawings are completed, ask students to locate on one of the maps where the event took place. Have the student who answers correctly tack his or her drawing to the appropriate state or country. This way, students will be able to see at a glance where important current events are taking place.

GAILE SENETTE

Pass The Globe

Pass the Globe is a game to play with students to encourage instruction during transition periods in the class schedule. It is an excellent way to teach or reinforce geography lessons to both elementary and intermediate students.

The only materials needed to play this game are a 16-inch globe that sits on a removable base and a rug large enough for the entire class to sit around the edge.

The teacher acts as the game leader. The teacher holds out the globe, calls the name of one student and rolls the globe across the rug to the student. Only the student whose name was called is permitted to touch the globe, preventing conflicts between students over whose turn it is.

The teacher asks the student a "globe" question, such as "Can you find North and South America on the globe?" If the student can answer the question correctly, he or she shows the place on the globe to the group. If the student's response is correct, the teacher says, "Pass the globe." The student then passes the globe across the rug to the student of his or her choice.

If the student cannot answer the question, he or she must roll the globe back to the teacher. The student can only "pass the globe" to another student if he or she gives the correct answer to the question.

This rule encourages students to pay attention to each other's answers and learn from the responses.

Game questions can be changed with the seasons and different units of study.

The game is also an opportunity for students to review for a geography or social studies test.

JUDY BRITT

Global Games

Use an inflatable globe to reinforce geography facts and motivate students to think quickly. Have the children stand in a circle. Call out a continent or country and gently toss the globe to one of the students. When the student catches the globe, he or she must point to the country or continent you called out. The student then gets to name a place on the globe and toss it to another student. Play should continue until every student has had a chance to catch the globe. For older students, you may want to designate a time limit for answers.

BRENDA H. MCGEE

The World

A Trip Around The World

To add visual interest to students' research reports on foreign countries, try this activity.

Right before pupils are ready to present their reports, have each presenter locate his or her given country on a large world map and mark it with a push pin. As the class' world travels begin, stretch yarn from country to country, indicating how the journey is progressing. Mileage and means of transportation could also be discussed. When the entire trip has been completed, photocopy all reports and bind them together into a Trip Around the World book.　CAROL CAPUTO

Things From Around The World

Ask your kids to participate in a "worldly" project to track down the origins of foreign products. Students check their clothing labels to find manufacturing locations. Locate these places on a world map and encourage children to speculate about how the items arrived in your area. Next, ask kids to look through their kitchen cupboards at home. Are any food products from out of the country? Mark these spots on your map, too. And finally, investigate the origins of toys, appliances, even cars. Help kids develop a growing awareness of the different forms of international influence on our lives.

BEATRICE BACHRACH PERRI

Social Studies Bingo

Here's an enjoyable way for kids to review social studies information. Give each student a copy of a blank bingo card — with four squares across and four squares down. Then, on the chalkboard, write 16 review items, such as geographic terms, important places and dates, or famous names. Kids copy words from the board, randomly placing one word in each blank on their cards. When students have filled in all the squares, choose one of the listed words and identify it by giving a descriptive clue or definition. Each time you give a clue, students put a marker — such as paper circles, buttons, pennies — on the square they think contains the target word. The first to correctly get four in a row — across, diagonally, or down — wins.

VICKIE MCCARTHY

Around The World In 80 Days

To inspire kids to learn more about geography, plan a trip around the world. Start on the first day of school and continue for the next 80 days. First, select an assortment of books on world holidays to display in your room. Encourage students to browse through the books and have each child choose several world holidays or events to research. Hand out index cards and have students write short paragraphs about their special occasions, including the date and country of origin. After kids have completed this task, collect the cards and arrange them in chronological order. Stack the cards in a special box titled "Around the World in 80 Days" and display at the front of the room. At the beginning of each day, call a student up to the box and ask him or her to read the day's holiday card and find the country on the map. Follow up with a brief discussion on where the holiday originated and how it's celebrated.　ALICE RICE

History

Time Travelers

Stimulate thinking about history with this "time machine" made from a large appliance carton. Cut a kids'-height opening through both sides. Decorate your machine with key dates in history, with time and travel-related words, and with symbols that conjure up time-travel images. Attach a supply of file cards for kids to record their time travels.

Ask each child to write an historical event — a discovery, an invention, the birth of a famous person — on one side of the file card. On the top of the card, he or she writes the date of the event — the actual date or a guess. Students then enter the "time machine" on their way to the library. At the library, kids locate three facts about the event, verify the correct date, and record the information on the back of the time card. When time travelers return to the present, ask each to share what they've learned with classmates. When all travels are completed, ask kids to arrange the individual cards in sequence to build a class time line.

JOAN KAMM

Comic History

Kids bring history's events to life with this cartoon activity. To begin, ask students to bring in comic strips. Point out basic cartoon features — characters, background illustration, balloon dialogue.

Now review events from a particular period in history and help kids break down events into scenes that could be presented in two or three panels. Each child decides on appropriate characters to include and ideas to express. Encourage research into details of clothing and architecture of the period for accurate illustrations. Display each child's completed work for peers to enjoy.

LEE WESTBROCK

Step Back In Time

"Good morning, I understand you're learning about the Declaration of Independence. The ideas weren't all mine, but I did write it."

Thomas Jefferson tips his hat and speaks to the spellbound class.

Sound far-fetched? It's not, with the help of a good costume and a teacher who enjoys acting.

Character portrayals can help teach an important concept. The teacher approaches the subject from what might have been the character's viewpoint.

Portraying an historical character requires research to actually "become" that person. Costumes can be simple or complex, depending on individual preference.

Character portrayals are exciting for students because they get information from a "personal" perspective. Students also learn that history involves people, not just facts, making the subject exciting.

Students can do their own character portrayals.

LYN JENKINS

Using Historical Documents

Report Card   **Student** <u>Suzanne Banning</u>

School Year—September 1936-June 1937

PROGRESS IN SCHOOL SUBJECTS	1	2	3	4
English	A	S	S	S
Reading	S	S	S	S
Social Studies	A	A	A	A
General Science	A	A	A	A
Latin	S	S	S	S
Music	F	A	A	A
Home Economics—Food/Clothing	S	A	S	S
Industrial Arts—Woodworking/Electricity/Metal				
Physical Education	A	A	A	
PROGRESS IN HABITS AND ATTITUDES				
1. Has neat appearance, is clean, shows evidence of sufficient sleep, has good posture	F	A	A	A
2. Keeps desk neat	F	F	F	F
3. Obeys promply and cheerfully	A	S	S	S
4. Considers rights of others	S	S	S	S
5. Is courteous	S	S	S	S
6. Accepts responsibility without supervision	A	S	S	S
7. Has good study habits	S	S	S	S
8. Uses leisure time wisely	A	A	S	S
9. Exercises self control in assemblies	F	F	A	A
10. Home room citizenship	F	A	A	S

Quarterly Period above columns 1 2 3 4

EXPLANATION OF RATINGS: F: Unsatisfactory   A: Satisfactory   S: Exceptional

Because they provide such powerful hands-on links with the past, historical documents can transport students to another time, another life, or another place. These documents can take many forms, from cherished declarations to those spun out of ordinary lives. This reproduction is of an elementary school student's report card for 1936-37. Use the activities here to guide students' exploration of what this document reveals about the girl who received it and the society she inhabited.

1. This report card grades students on school subjects and behavior. Find three academic subjects that students are still graded on today.

2. Name four qualities that teachers in the 1930's seemed to value highly. Are these qualities valued today as well? Why or why not?

3. The virtues fall into several categories. Which have to do with interactions among classmates? Which concern how students relate to teachers or other adults? Which have to do with controlling one's behavior? And which reflect a child's home life?

4. Most schools are concerned with preparing students to meet the challenges they'll face as adults in the working world. What subjects did schools emphasize in 1937? What subjects do you study today to prepare yourself for life in the next century?

5. Interview an adult about the kind of report card he or she received as a child. See if you can borrow an old report card and bring it to class. Does it differ from the one you receive today? From the one in 1937?

6. Write a paragraph describing the student who received this report card. What are her best and worst qualities? What do you think she did in her spare time? What job do you think she held as an adult?

7. In 1937, students received two grades for each subject — one for how hard they worked, and one for how much they achieved. Would you prefer a grading system like this? Why or why not?

CAROLYN HARDESTY

History

The Great Debate

Conduct an informal debate using topics from previous decades that were once considered controversial. For example, have students debate issues such as, Should women work? Is space travel possible? Is rock and roll harmful to kids? Should Alaska and Hawaii be admitted as states to the Union? Encourage children to research their chosen subject by interviewing family members, relatives, and neighbors who remember when the issue was hot. When it's time to debate, children would argue their topics from a past point of reference. For example, if the topic is women's suffrage, children should argue as if they are actually from this time period. This allows them to consider the spirit of the issue since they must try to put themselves in the shoes of those who were involved in the original debate. Whether the topic is serious or somewhat silly, students must do some creative thinking — while having lots of fun in the process.

JULIE S. POLAK

Research The Holidays

Investigate the moods and values of our country in history by researching some of our national holidays. Have student committees select a non-religious holiday or special day of observance such as Veteran's Day, Memorial Day, Fire Prevention Week, Earth Day, Fourth of July, Flag Day, and so on and research its history. Find out why the day was created, why that particular date was chosen, when the observance was enacted, who instigated it, and so on.

Once all information has been collected, committees can report to the rest of the class. After each report, discuss what the day tells about the interests of the country at that time.

When all reports have been made, create a bulletin board time line with the holidays plotted on it. Which day was the first to be celebrated? What is the newest observance?

You Are There

Have students choose a person from American history and research his or her life. Ask each pupil to read at least two books (or other relevant materials) on the individual and take notes, in order to become familiar with the person's life and accomplishments. When each child knows his or her famous person inside and out, have the child dress in appropriate costume to be interviewed by the class. Or have two "famous people" from different time periods engage in conversation and give one another information about their customs and cultures.

BRUCE LUND

A Name Game

Here's a quick memory game for reviewing notable names from class units on history, literature, or current events. Ask students to list six sets of initials, then to exchange papers. Kids write down the name of a famous person who fits each set of initials.

ISOBEL LIVINGSTONE

The Election Process

Tune In And Turn Kids On With Election Watch

Awaken students to citizenship responsibilities by stressing active observation in the election process. These activities can heighten awareness and interest in the political process. Plan them for the period preceding a major election.

Recording Events

Ask students to keep scrapbooks of newspaper articles concerning elections and candidates and campaign journals. Have them watch the news each evening and use their note-taking skills to record election coverage. At school the next day, ask them to write an entry in their journal paraphrasing their notes.

Create a list of campaign issues and ask students to record the candidates' positions on them. Students might enjoy creating a chart to compare the candidates' positions and statements on key issues.

Have students collect graphs and poll results from magazines, newspapers and television newscasts. Use a bulletin board or a section of the chalkboard to record the poll results. In a math lesson, explain interpretation of polling results and the importance of margin of error. Describe different types of survey techniques, such as telephone and personal interviews and exit polls.

Contact your local newspaper and arrange to purchase papers for your class for the week before the election and two days after it.

Background

Ask students to research and write biographies of the candidates. Have students take turns role-playing the candidates while others interview them in a news conference. Interviews can include questions on the candidates' backgrounds as well as current campaign events. Alternate this type of interview with "Face the Nation" or "Meet the Press" approaches in the weeks before the election.

Lampooning and Cartooning

Explain political cartoons. You might include historical examples from earlier election campaigns. Your discussion could include stereotypes ("Uncle Sam," Washington politicians, nations and so on) and caricatures. Ask students to draw their own cartoons or to keep a section of their scrapbooks for campaign-related cartoons.

Suggest that students choose one cartoonist to read regularly; ask them to observe differences in the renderings or the cartoonist's attitude toward the candidates.

Invite the cartoonist from the local newspaper to visit your class to talk about his art.

Political Organization

Arrange a phone call or a visit to a campaign headquarters. Ask students to compile a list of campaign jobs and responsibilities. To do so, they should interview as many campaign workers, from managers to phone solicitors, as possible.

Write to an election headquarters and request buttons, bumper stickers and literature.

Invite political figures to visit your class. Former politicians can give special insights about government and campaigning.

Advertising

Ask your class to keep a record of the types of ads — print, radio, television, or billboard — they see or hear for each candidate. Ask students to think about how the ad works: How does it try to persuade the audience to vote for the candidate? Does it use endorsements or generalities to elicit support? You might request political advertising rates from local media or ask the advertising managers to send a speaker to discuss political advertising.

Watching The Race

If this is a presidential year, create a map that shows the number of electoral votes in each state or territory. Introduce the electoral college and ask students to suggest other methods, such as popular vote, to elect a president. Stage a debate to present the advantages and disadvantages of a popular vote versus the electoral college.

Before the election, record poll results from newspaper, magazine or television reports to show which candidate is expected to win in each state and the expected victory margin. After the election, ask students to put the popular vote on the map. LINDA HOLLINGSWORTH-BROWN

The Election Process

Vote Dinosaurs

Capitalize on primary youngsters' interest in dinosaurs with a mascot election that introduces the election process.

Use the winner for a stationery or newsletter logo for your classroom. Or expand the election to a grade level or school mascot competition.

Supplement your activities with trips to local museums, guest speakers and reading materials.

Assigning Parties

Begin election activities by discussing the qualities — bravery, friendliness, strength, ferociousness — students think a school mascot should have.

Then introduce students to the six species of dinosaurs on the reproducible, or select your own. Explain to students that these unusual creatures lived millions of years ago during the Mesozoic Era, which is divided into three periods: the Jurassic, Triassic and Cretaceous (see reproducible).

During these periods, a variety of dinosaurs with different characteristics — from relatively small animals the size of ostriches, to massive creatures as tall as four-story buildings — lived on earth.

To start the election activities, explain that, despite their differences, dinosaurs generally belong to one of two groups: meat eaters (carnivores) or plant eaters (herbivores).

Randomly assign students to meat eater or plant eater parties. Ask each party to select a name (Veggies, Herbicans, Meat Munchers, Carnicrats).

Explain that each party will select a candidate to run for mascot, but to vote, students must register.

Voter Registration

Ask students to write their names and addresses on 3-by 5-inch cards and return them to you. Design symbols for each party and attach them to the appropriate cards.

To register students, ask them to come to a special area where you or an aide checks their name on your class list. Return their cards. Tell them to show the card before voting to verify their registration.

Primary Election

Students will vote for a candidate from the three dinosaurs running from their party. Ask them to select the one they think will be the best leader.

Make a voting booth from a refrigerator box or a desk carrel to create an area where students can vote in privacy. Ask a student from each party to check that students have registration cards and pick up only one ballot. Explain that a secret ballot means no one has to know for whom they vote because they don't sign their names and they vote in privacy. Ask students to put their ballots in a ballot box, which can be made from a shoe box.

Following the vote, announce the winners.

Campaigning

Explain that a campaign makes voters aware of a candidate's qualifications. Give party members assignments, such as campaign manager or press agent. Ask students to suggest duties.

Activities:

• Make a poster-sized calendar with election events. Circle November 8 for the general election.

• Let students put out an election newsletter with background about the candidates and important election dates.

• Make campaign buttons, bumper stickers, posters and murals.

• Make dinosaur hats for students to wear at the rally.

• Write campaign songs, chants and slogans

• Ask each party to write a platform that presents the candidate's views on campaign issues.

• Hold a rally by selecting a student from each party to speak for the candidate. Help them prepare speeches about the party platform and their qualifications. Let party members chant slogans, sing songs and wave placards. Ask music teachers, parents and aides to help decorate.

General Election and Victory Party

Hold the election in a designated voting area in the morning. Ask students to bring their registration cards and vote, again by secret ballot, for their choice. Count the votes, announce the winner and celebrate a victory in the afternoon.

BETTY FRY

Primary Election Ballot _____

Plant Eaters

Place an X in the box next to the plant-eating dinosaur you want for mascot.

Brachiosaurus
Jurassic Period
(180 to 130 million years ago)

The largest dinosaur, Brachiosaurus, weighed about 85 tons, stood about 40 feet high and was about 70 feet long. It had a short tail and a long neck. These "armlizards" probably moved very slowly—about two to three miles an hour. Like a giraffe, its front legs were longer than its back legs.

Stegosaurus
Jurassic Period
(180 to 130 million years ago)

The Plated Stegosaurus walked on four legs and was about the height of an elephant—approximately 11 feet high. With its heavy tail, it was about 25 feet long. Its back legs were longer than its front legs, and it had a vertical series of bony plates along the middle of its back and spikes on its thick tail. The Stegosaurus lived in herds and fed on low plants.

Triceratops
Cretaceous Period
(130 to 65 million years ago)

Like a rhinoceros, the Triceratops had a huge head. It weighed 8 to 9 tons—about the same as an elephant—but it was shorter. This horned creature had a long, heavy tail and a heavy neck shield. On its face were three horns: a short one on its nose and one over each eye. The horns above the eyes grew up to 3 feet long.

Meat Eaters

Place an X in the box next to the meat-eating dinosaur you want for mascot.

Tyrannosaurs rex
Cretaceous Period
(130 to 65 million years ago)

The most feared of all dinosaurs, Tyrannosaurs rex ruled the land at the end of the age of reptiles. Its head measured up to 4 feet and is length ranged to 40 feet. Standing upright, it was about 10 feet tall at the hips. This "terrible lizard" walked upright like a person. Its two short forelimbs were weak, but its teeth were each about an inch wide and serrated like knives.

Deinonychus
Cretaceous Period
(130 to 65 million years ago)

Deinonychus, probably the fiercest dinosaur, stood about 3 to 5 feet tall, weighed about 150 to 175 pounds and had a large, curved claw on each foot. It used these 5-inch claws as weapons. The small, quick beast may have lived and hunted in packs, like the wolf.

Ornitholestes
Jurassic Period
(180 to 130 million years ago)

About 5 to 6 feet long with a 3-foot tail, this creature moved on two legs and had sharp claws. Its name, "bird robber," would make you think it probably ate any small game. The short arms of the Ornitholestes had three fingers that it probably used in hunting.

5 Science

Introduction

For many teachers, the subject they feel is more difficult to teach is science. Yet, many schools do not supply textbooks so teachers must create their own science programs. For those teachers, here are experiments, observations, examples of simple chemical and physical changes — making it easier to plan and carry out interesting classroom activities.

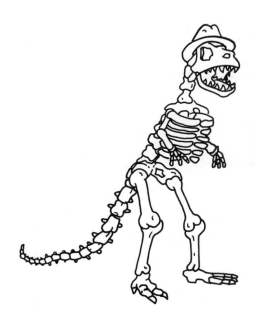

First Grade Tools

Limited ability to write need not hamper young learners in recording science observations. A date stamp found in school libraries makes a handy record-keeping tool. Set aside a daily observation period when studying plants, tadpoles, etc. Have students stamp the date and record a brief observation. Periodically ask students to refer to their notebooks, asking questions such as "When did the tadpole's legs first appear?" to point out the value of scientific record-keeping.

Some youngsters are capable of in-depth research. Use the school copier (within reason) to allow these students to gather information to paste in their notebooks. PAULA DICKINSON

Dry Bones Make A Real Rex

Invite Tyrannosaurus Rex to your classroom for an exercise in visual/perception matching. Build your own small model using bleached turkey bones.

Trace an outline of the bone arrangement on construction paper. Encourage children to match pieces to the drawing. To motivate children, start with Rex preassembled. Children can mess it up and reassemble the puzzle.
TERESA THOMPSON

Science Concepts

Edible Atoms

Illustrate the relationships of the parts of the atom using gumdrops for nuclei, marshmallows for electrons, and toothpicks for the orbits of the electrons. Start by giving each student a sandwich bag with one large gumdrop, three toothpicks, and six miniature marshmallows. Kids push toothpicks diagonally through their gumdrops from bottom to top, so that the gumdrops stand on their own tripods. Students then stick marshmallows on the end of each toothpick. When they add the last marshmallow, each child has a simple model of the atom!

Use the models to explain the relationship of the nuclei — made up of protons and neutrons — to the electrons. Then end the lesson the way kids might hope — let them eat their atoms!

JAN BRIGHT

More Evidence, Please

Here's an activity that helps children develop scientific process skills.

First set up a slide projector in your classroom. Choose a color slide to project onto the wall and show the picture badly out of focus. Next, ask students to infer what the picture might be. What observations led them to draw these conclusions? Then focus the picture slightly and invite students to share what new evidence they have gathered. Allow each child to change his or her original inference. Continue focusing the picture until it is clear. Have pupils compare their original inferences with the picture, then follow up with a class discussion on the importance and value of employing the scientific process in all disciplines.

LORRAINE UPTON

Grow Your Own Germs

You can illustrate, memorably, the presence of germs everywhere, with a few slices of potato. Divide the class into groups. Provide three slices of raw potato per group. Hand the first slice around the group and encourage each member to handle it extensively. Pass the second piece around and have children blow on it without touching it. The third slice can be used to clean the blackboard, the floor, desk tops. Place potato slices in individual self-closing bags, label and put in a dark closet for a week. Children will be amazed and horrified when they see what has grown on the potato slices.   MARILYN BENNETT

Fry An Egg

Is it hot enough to fry an egg? This may be an old question, but the answer gives a great example of a scientific principle.

It is necessary to choose a warm day for this experiment.

The procedure for the experiment is as follows:

1. Crack an egg into a black skillet.
2. Crack an egg into a white skillet. (If you don't have a white skillet, spray paint an old skillet white.)
3. Place the skillets in an area outside where they will not be tampered with throughout the day.
4. Check the skillets periodically.

Usually by noon the results will be in. The black skillet will cook the egg faster than the white skillet.

This reinforces the fact that black absorbs heat faster than white.   ELLEN SMITH

Simple Science Projects

Sensory Boxes

Culminate a unit on the senses by helping students challenge classmates' sense of touch with mystery boxes.

Each child first secretly selects an object that has no sharp edges or points — a feather, popcorn kernels, Velcro strip, lemon, plastic foam, sandpaper, pinecone, cotton ball, seashell, or marshmallow — then brings the item to school in a shoe box. Kids cover their boxes with colored paper and use markers to write intriguing questions on the sides and top. Assist each child in cutting a four-inch-wide hole — large enough for a hand to fit through — in one side of the box.

Now find a place around the room for each child to set up a "mystery center." Each places his or her box in front of a 24- by 18-inch poster. On one side of the poster, the child lists properties of the mystery item. On the other side he or she staples an original story about the mystery item.

When centers are complete, invite students to test their sense of touch by visiting each one.   JOAN KAMM

Science Scale

Stock your science shelf with a balance scale made from a clothes hanger, two aluminum pie plates, and some string. First, poke three holes in each pie plate — at four, eight, and 12 o'clock positions. Tie a length of string through each hole. Fasten one plate to each end of the hanger so that each hangs six inches. Attach hanger to a hook or over a chair so the balance swings freely. Kids weigh objects using paper clips or pennies as standard units.
                                                                                                                              DOROTHY ZJAWIN

What Am I?

Create an intriguing bulletin board display, fun science activity or learning center with these easy-to-do animal research projects.

Have each student glue a picture of an animal to a piece of construction paper. Staple another piece of paper the same size to the top edge of this paper. Cut a hole in the top paper to reveal a small portion of the picture underneath.

The student then writes several clues to the identity of the animal on the top piece of paper. Using the clues, classmates try to guess what animal is pictured. They lift the top piece of paper to see if their guesses are correct.
                                                     MARY ANN BRENSEL

Bird Count

Enhance your study of local ecology with an official bird count. You'll encourage students to be more aware of bird habitats and bird behavior.

First, call on a local Audubon Society member or an experienced bird watcher to help identify birds most likely to be seen in your area. Before the count begins, encourage students to research different birds on the list.

Give each child a copy of the bird list. Kids mark each time they see a bird. Daily, combine student tallies on a master list posted in the classroom. At the end of three weeks, total the marks for each type of bird, then discuss with kids what the count reveals about the bird population in your area.   JUDY NICHOLS

Plants

Adopt A Tree

Have your students become partners with nature. Ask the class to choose a tree in the school yard or neighborhood to adopt. They will study the tree, and, along with nature, help it thrive.

First, take the class on a walk around the school to look at possible candidates for adoption. Create a nominating committee and conduct a vote for the tree.

Once selected, the class may wish to label the tree temporarily to indicate it has been adopted. Attach a sign with twine or masking tape so that the tree isn't harmed, or place a sign in the ground.

Make a list of questions for students to answer about the tree so they can get to know it. Students answer the questions by observing the tree and doing research. Ask them to describe the tree; its buds; evidence of disease; clues that animals may be using the tree; any plants growing on the tree; changes that take place in the tree throughout the year; the purpose of its leaves, roots, bark, trunk, buds, flowers, etc.; how the tree gets food and water, etc. Ask the students to measure the diameter of the trunk and estimate the tree's age and height. After students are familiar with the tree, try some of the following activities:
• Make a crayon bark rubbing.
• Photograph your tree through the seasons and make a display.
• Have a party for the tree.
• Make a model of the tree.
• Make a certificate officially recognizing the adoption of the tree.
• Write poems about the tree.
• Ask a forester or tree expert to visit the class and discuss trees and their proper care. Have the class prune and fertilize the tree, and attend to any of its other needs.
• Write a story about a typical day in the life of your tree.
• Conduct a class period under the tree.

MARK JENNES

Pop-Bottle Terrariums

Keep those disposable 2-liter plastic soda bottles and recycle them into individual terrariums. The process is simple.
1. Pour a few inches of hot water into the bottle. Allow it to set for a few minutes to loosen the glue holding the base.
2. Carefully remove the colored-plastic base from the bottle. Work slowly to avoid cracking the base.
3. Clean any remaining glue off the bottle.
4. Use a sharp knife or scissors to cut the top off the bottle as shown in the diagram
5. Place a layer of drainage material — sand, fish gravel, charcoal chips, or pebbles — in the bottom of the base.
6. Add soil, preferably containing some charcoal.
7. Add plants, lichens, and moss. Choose plants that require the same amount of light and that grow slowly.
8. Slowly add water to the soil and mist the foliage. Observe the terrarium closely for a few days to see if it needs more water. Add extra water if required.

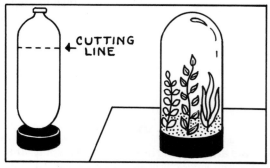

9. Cover the terrarium with the plastic dome you created from the rest of the bottle. Keep it in the shade for a few days to allow the plants to settle in. Check the dome each day for condensation. If there is none on the top and sides of the dome, you will need to add water. If condensation is heavy, there is too much water in the terrarium. Wipe the condensation off the dome daily until the moisture content is corrected.
10. Some bottles have bases with holes in them. If your terrarium is made from one of these, place it on a saucer to catch the excess water.

KELLY RILEY

Animals

Homing In On Habitats

Help your class think about how animals and plants adapt to their homes with these activities.

Habitat Sort

List habitats on one side of the board, animals and plants on the other. Ask students to connect each living thing to its natural home:

jungle	polar bear
forest	frog
pond	cactus
river	whale
ocean	salmon
arctic	monkey
desert	maple tree

Ask older students to make up their own habitat sort game, using the same habitats but new plants and animals.

Animals By Design

Have each student make up an animal that might live in one of these habitats: arctic tundra, mountain, ocean, lake, prairie, beach, forest, river, jungle. They should draw their animal in its habitat, name the new "species" and describe the way it adapts to the habitat.

What Makes A Home?

Ask students to list what is needed for a habitat to support life. Then explain that all habitats provide water, air, food and shelter. Give students the names of several habitats and explain how they meet these needs.

Wild Scavenger Hunt

Let students examine their own habitat by looking for one of each item on this list: things that are green, brown, once alive, never alive, soft, hard, round, smooth, older than they are, younger than they are, man-made, things that can be burned, can be eaten, cannot be eaten. Ask older students to see who can find the most of each.

Predator And Prey

An animal that seeks out other animals to eat is called a predator; the animal trying to hide and protect itself is the prey. Ask students to think of several predator-prey pairs: cat-bird, bear-fish, wolf-caribou or bird-insect. Have the class play an outdoor game of "Predator and Prey" modeled on "Hide and Seek." Let one or two choose what predator they will be and stalk the rest. After the game, ask the prey what strategies these animals might use to try to avoid the predator, for instance, stinging, biting, running away and so on.

Librarian's Habitat

Give one group of students a list of animals. Let them choose an animal from the list and write a short report describing its habitat and the adaptations the animal has made to the habitat. The list could include: pika, desert fox, snowshoe rabbit, sea lion, amoeba, buffalo, sea gull, elephant, pigeon and beaver.

Give another group clues about a "mystery animal" and direct them to particular books in which they'll be able to find the animal. Ask them to describe its habitat. For example, give these clues: a bird, black and white, lives in Antarctica, eats fish. Students should say this is a penguin that lives in an arctic habitat.

What Happened Here?

Have students fold a sheet of paper into thirds as shown. On the left third of the page have them draw two sets of animal tracks leading to the middle third of the paper. In the middle of the page have them draw a jumble of tracks as though the animals had met. On the right third of the paper ask them to show only one animal's tracks leaving the scene. Ask them to write a story explaining the sequence of events implied by the tracks. Answers will vary; the more imaginative, the better.

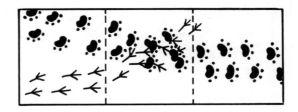

Potato Paw Prints

Let students use potato halves to create animal-like tracks. Pictures of actual animal tracks will probably inspire some fanciful animals. Let two students work together to print their tracks, making up a new animal track story as they do.

LAUREL SHERMAN

Show what you know

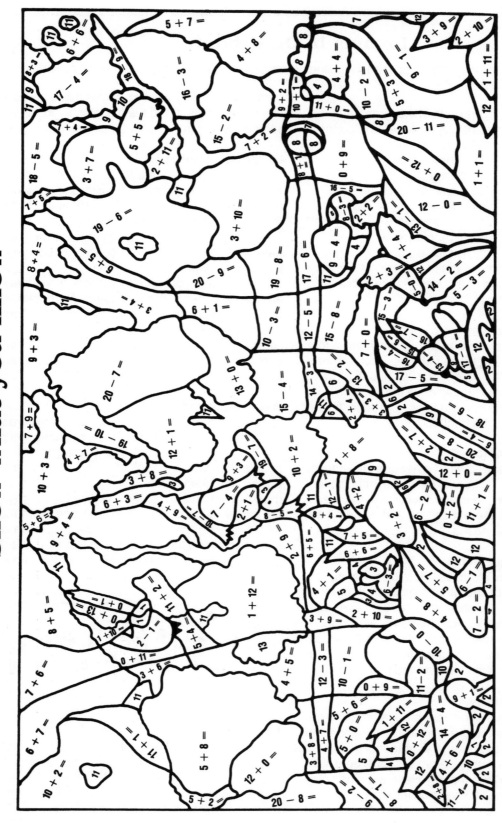

Animals Hidden In The Forest

There are nine animals hidden in this forest. To find them you will answer each math problem and then color the spaces. Every time you find a problem whose sum or difference is 3, for example, you will color the space grey.

Did you find these animals? squirrel, mouse, butterfly, fox, deer, rabbit, opossum, bear, bird

1 dark blue	**9** tan
2 dark gree	**10** orange
3 grey	**11** light blue
4 brown	**12** yellow green
5 yellow	**13** green
6 burnt sienna	Unnumbered spaces
7 dark brown	should be colored
8 black	white or left colorless.

Weather

BEAUFORT SCALE OF WINDS			
Beaufort Number	Name of Wind	Effects of Wind	MPH
0	Calm	Smoke rises straight up.	Less than 1
1	Light air	Smoke drifts gently. Wind vane still.	1-3
2	Light breeze	Face feels wind. Leaves rustle.	4-7
3	Gentle breeze	Leaves and small twigs move.	8-12
4	Moderate breeze	Stirs dust, paper, and small branches.	13-18
5	Fresh breeze	Small trees sway. Wavelets on lakes.	19-24
6	Strong breeze	Branches move. Wind sound in wires.	25-31
7	Moderate gale	Whole trees move. Walking dificult.	32-38
8	Fresh gale	Twigs broken off.	39-46
9	Strong gale	Loose shingles and chimneys go.	47-54
10	Whole gale	Trees uprooted.	55-63
11	Storm	Widespread damage.	64-72
12	Hurricane	Anything may go.	Above 72

It's In The Wind

Give students a feel for interpreting the significance of wind speeds, and acquaint them with "wind words" such as breeze, gale, storm, and hurricane. Use the Beaufort Wind Scale as the basis for quiz games with questions such as: What physical evidence do you associate with 35 mph winds? (Walking is difficult and whole trees seem to move.) Or, according to the Beaufort Scale, what is the name of the wind that causes smoke to go straight up? (Calm)

Try a matching exercise. Kids match the wind activity with the proper speed: You see little waves on the lake (19-24 mph). Pieces of a roof are flying off (47-54 mph).

After students are familiar with the scale, talk about windchill factors and charts. Extend your study to wind disasters such as blizzards, chinooks, cyclones, hurricanes, tornados, and typhoons, and specific rules of safety.

BEATRICE BACKRACH PERRI

Weather Calendars

Make a weather wall calendar for each month of the year. Mark each day with the appropriate weather symbol, then calculate the totals for snowy days, sunny days, and so on at the end of the month. Use monthly and end-of-the-year totals to teach children how to make graphs.

PRISCILLA OLMSTED

Weather Watch

Students confirm the change of seasons in this science observation activity. Each day, ask children to record the temperature of a thermometer placed in a shady spot outside your classroom window or on the playground. Students transfer temperature data to a graph, with horizontal lines for temperatures and vertical lines for days. After three weeks, ask kids what patterns they see in the data.

MILDRED THOMAS

The Sky Above

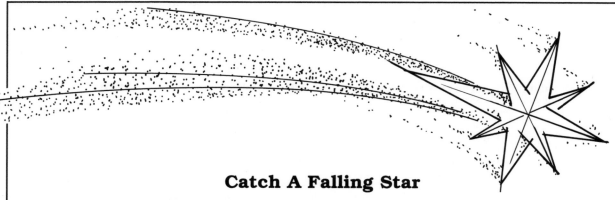

Catch A Falling Star

Three classes of sixth graders — about 80 students in all — and their families participated in Catch a Falling Star, an astronomy project developed by Jon Shade. Through a variety of activities, students and their families learned to recognize and identify constellations in the Pennsylvania sky. Some of the activities even encouraged students to rearrange the night sky.

One popular activity had students create their own constellations. First, students drew imaginary constellations on cardboard. Then, with their parents' help, they developed mythologies to explain the origins of their constellations. Finally, classes worked together to assemble the individual constellations into an imaginary night sky.

Some families tie-dyed constellations onto T-shirts. Others found old slides of stars, pricked them with pins, and projected new constellations on a wall or screen. And others used 12-inch diameter salad bowls to create miniature planetariums. They turned the bowls upside down over low-wattage bulbs, drilled holes to correspond to constellations, and projected the images on the wall. Finally, some students "decked the halls" with miniature Christmas lights, covering the lights with black paper, and, using pinpricks, created constellations.

Families gathered for star parties once a month, during which they gazed at real constellations.

To keep participants informed of upcoming events and activities, students produced a monthly newsletter that went home to parents. Each issue included a schedule of events, pointers for family star gazing, and tips on using binoculars to locate constellations.

ROBERT BURROUGHS

A Stellar Idea

Poke pinholes through slides that didn't develop properly to represent stars in constellations. Project on a wall or screen, then get ready for some "cosmic" fun!

BERTHA BRYANT

Space Panorama

A study of the solar system can lead to an interesting art activity. Have students spatter-paint large sheets of black construction paper with white tempera. The desired effect is the appearance of a galaxy. Let dry.

Have children make planets, stars, and comets from construction paper or aluminum foil, and glue them on to complete the picture.

DONNA LYNN BROWNING

Magnetism

The Magic Of Magnets

Children love to study magnetism. Here's a lively way to foster that learning: Give a magnet to each student in your class. Magnets with clips on them—available at drugstores—are especially easy for small hands to grasp. Instruct children to go around the room, see which objects the magnets attract, and write them down. (If you like, you can turn this activity into a game by giving children a point for each object they can locate. The student with the most points wins!) After about ten minutes, have the students return to their seats. On the board, write the headings "Magnets Attract" and "Magnets Do Not Attract." Then, using the students' data, create a class list of objects such as paperclips, metal safety scissors, metal desk, etc.

After your list is complete, discuss magnetism. What objects did the magnets attract? What do the objects have in common? Help your students to conclude that magnets only attract metal objects. Then, using an encyclopedia or science book, investigate further. Help your students to understand that magnets get their special power from tiny molecules—each a tiny magnet—which are all lined up and pull in the same direction. Regular metals are made up of molecules, too, but those are scattered and pull in different directions.

After the class has gained insight into magnetism, use the topic as a springboard for creative writing. Ask your class to anthropomorphize (give human characteristics to) a magnet, and write a story entitled "Marvin the Magnet's Big Adventure." Or, they can write a rhyming poem about the special things that magnets attract.

Radical Rice

As the air outside gets colder and drier, your students may notice their hair sticking to their hats when they come inside from recess. When that happens, try this simple experiment to demonstrate static electricity. You'll need aluminum foil, a plastic container with a clear lid, bits of puffed rice cereal, and a piece of woolen fabric. Cut a circle of foil that's six inches larger in diameter than the container. Use your fingertips to depress the foil about an inch. Scatter small bits of puffed rice on the foil and cover it with the plastic lid. Briskly rub the woolen fabric over the container's lid and watch the rice rise and fall. Explain to the class that the wool creates a negative charge on the lid, which attracts the uncharged rice. When the rice hits the lid, it also becomes negatively charged and is repelled.

ELLEN SMITH

Chemistry

Kitchen Cupboard Chemistry

Common household items help teach children principles of chemistry. These examples use flour, sugar, salt, baking soda, vinegar, rubbing alcohol, food coloring, liquid soap, Epsom salts, and Polident tablets.

Look-alike Chemicals Many chemicals that look the same are actually quite different. Have children study and feel flour, baking soda, sugar, salt, and Epsom salts, and try to identify the differences. (Flour and baking soda are powders; sugar, salt, and Epsom salts are crystals.) Now have kids observe differences in some clear liquids: water, vinegar, rubbing alcohol. (Water is odorless; vinegar and alcohol have strong odors.)

Bubble and Fizz When certain chemicals combine, they react in two special ways: by bubbling or by fizzing. Drop a Polident tablet in a cup of water; as the tablet dissolves, bubbles form and rise to the surface. (To make bubbling occur faster, use warm water or break the tablet into small pieces; to make it occur more slowly, use cold water.) Now add a spoonful of baking soda to vinegar and

watch it fizz. Add a spoonful of flour to vinegar and note that it doesn't fizz. Put samples of baking soda and flour in unmarked containers and use the vinegar fizz test to identify each.

You can create an exciting bubbling foam with just four chemicals. Fill a glass jar half full with vinegar, add six drops of liquid soap, five drops of green food coloring, and two spoonfuls of baking soda. The fizz caused by adding baking soda to vinegar causes the liquid soap to bubble and combine with the food coloring. This chemical change makes green bubbling foam rise from the jar and spill down the sides.

KATHERINE LEATHERS

Chemical Stripes

Demonstrate that liquids have different densities — some are heavier than water and some are lighter — with this experiment. You'll need corn syrup, yellow cooking oil, water, food coloring, wax paper, plastic cups, a small jar for each child, and paper towels.

First, you'll need to prepare some of the materials. Color a bottle of corn syrup blue by stirring in several drops of food coloring. Add drops of red food coloring to a jar of water. Now pour the corn syrup, water, and cooking oil into plastic cups. Divide children into groups of three or four and provide each group with one cup of each liquid. Give each child a piece of wax paper and a jar.

Tell kids that they are going to examine some liquids. Ask students to dip their fingers in the red liquid and to place a few drops on the wax paper. Ask them to rub fingers together and to describe how the liquid feels. Then ask students to observe the drops of red liquid on the wax paper and to try to move the drops around using their fingers. Encourage kids to describe what they see and feel. Finally, ask them if they can guess what the red liquid is, then reveal that it's water. Repeat the same procedure using the corn syrup, then the cooking oil.

Now tell children that they are going to create liquid stripes in their jars. First, ask kids to fill their jars half full with the red water. Ask them to predict what will happen when they add the blue corn syrup, then tell them to pour a small amount of the liquid into their jars. Ask kids to describe and explain what happens. (The corn syrup will flow to the bottom of the jar because it's more dense than the water.) Finally, ask kids to repeat the process with cooking oil. (The cooking oil will float on top of the water because it's less dense.)

STEPHEN BLUME

Chemistry

Pseudo-Photography

"Photography" in the classroom? With no darkroom, no cameras and little money? Yes!

A chemigram is a convenient, fascinating way to introduce children to the three basic photo chemicals. Using few materials and an easy procedure allows images to materialize before your eyes.

Most black-and-white enlarging papers can be used under ordinary room light to achieve interesting "paintings." Use old, expired enlarging papers when you can — the results will be fine. The chemicals you need (developer, stop bath and fixer) are safe for children to use under teacher supervision and direction. Use tongs (large tweezers) to keep fingers out of the solutions. Mix the chemicals according to package directions.

You will need three trays, some cotton swabs and a sink or container of water. Give each student a sheet of photo paper and several cotton swabs. Let them apply developer to the paper in several areas, painting lines and shapes. Then watch in amazement as the designs appear like magic.

Next, place each paper in a tray containing stop bath. Tell the students this solution stops the action of the developer on their papers. Within a minute of so you can move the papers to a tray of fixer. Tell children that fixer clears the papers of the previous chemicals and makes the design permanent. Leave the papers in the fixer tray for four minutes or longer.

Finally, wash all the papers in water for about 10 minutes. If you have access to a sink, use running water.

For a variation, paint fixer on an exposed sheet of blank photo paper. Wait several moments, then process it with developer, stop bath, fixer again and water bath.
PAULA GUHIN

Weather An Eggshell

Try this experiment to help students understand the composition of limestone and marble.

Hard boil an egg, and place it in a jar filled with vinegar. Loosely cover the jar, and place it where students can observe it. Bubbles should be forming around the shell. Some bubbles leave the egg, and some remain attached to the egg, enabling it to float.

One day later remove the egg and rinse in water. The shell should have disappeared, leaving a leathery membrane covering the egg. The egg can be bounced like a ball.

Next, drop a piece of chalk into the vinegar. Bubbles will rise and pieces of the chalk will disappear. Pieces of limestone, marble and clamshells also make bubbles in vinegar.

Conclude that in acid, calcium carbonate (the major component of eggshells, limestone, marble, animal bones, clamshells and chalk) undergoes a chemical change. Through this reaction, carbon dioxide is separated from calcium carbonate. The carbon dioxide makes the bubbles. The remaining component, calcium acetate, dissolves.

Observing that the eggshell, clamshell, limestone and marble react similarly to acid will help students understand that these materials all contain calcium carbonate. Limestone and marble contain calcium carbonate because they were formed over time from sea animal remains millions of years ago.

Chemistry

Poltergeist Punch

Anytime your class studies states of matter, try this "haunted" punch experiment. You'll start with the macabre and finish with matter-of-fact scientific thinking. Have a volunteer who watches so no one is burned or hurt.

You'll need one large punch bowl filled with water. Surround the bowl with a dozen stubby candles, plus one or two tall ones. Light the candles. Then, wearing gloves, drop about 6 ounces of dry ice into the bowl. Dry ice is inexpensive and can be purchased at ice cream stores. Don't touch the dry ice unprotected. Its temperature of -78 degrees Centigrade will burn you.

Once the dry ice enters the bowl, the contents appear to be boiling. The liquid in the bowl is warming up the dry ice. Dry ice is carbon dioxide gas that has been frozen into a solid at very cold temperatures. When it warms up, it skips its liquid stage or sublimes — goes straight from a solid to a gas. Because carbon dioxide gas is less dense than water, the gas bubbles rush to the surface, making the water appear to boil.

What happens next? Steam appears to rise from this boiling cauldron. Actually, clouds are forming above it. The gas rising out of the liquid is very cold. It condenses the gaseous water in the air to liquid water, forming clouds like those in the sky.

Now the candles sputter out. The carbon dioxide gas has done it again. The gas is denser than air, so it sinks down and replaces the oxygen that the candles need in order to burn. Out they go except perhaps the tall candles, which are higher up, so are not overcome by the sinking carbon dioxide.

After you perform this experiment, the class can make its own carbon dioxide. Combine vinegar and baking soda. Or add Kool-Aid to the baking soda, then water. The weak acids in the Kook-Aid and vinegar break down the sodium bicarbonate in the baking soda, releasing carbon dioxide gas. Do kids realize that carbon dioxide is the fizz that's in soda pop? It's the same gas that we exhale and that plants need to make food.

MICKEY SARQUIS   BETTY KIBBEY

Molecule Madness

Teach the concept of molecular density in solids, liquids, and gases by letting kids pretend to be molecules.

To demonstrate molecular density and movement in a gas, students move around the room in a smooth and constant motion, arms outstretched. To demonstrate density and movement in a liquid, children crowd in a little closer, leaving just enough room to turn their bodies around with their hands at their sides. Fluidity in gases and liquids can be shown by a flowing movement through a doorway, with the shape of the mass changing as it goes. Movement and density in a solid are shown by crowding together as closely as possible while still trying to move.

JEFFREY FINKEL

Electric Lemons?

Maybe you can't get blood from a stone, but you can get a charge out of a lemon! Demonstrate the principle of the electric cell using an ordinary lemon; two strands of copper wire, each with clips on both ends; a penny and a dime; and a voltmeter.

Insert the coins into separate slits made in the lemon, then attach each copper wire to a coin and to the voltmeter. If the needle on the voltmeter jumps backwards, disconnect the meter and reverse the wires. After presenting this demonstration to students, ask them to hypothesize various ways to increase the voltage, such as changing the coins used.

RACHEL WEINTRAUB

6 Physical Education and Health

Introduction

While everyone recognizes that physical education and health are important parts of the curriculum, very often there are no spelled-out plans for teaching these subjects. Yet teachers must include them in their plans. These ideas for playground games, fitness activities, nutrition, dental health, safety, and good health practices are easily included in your daily teaching to become part of your curriculum.

Volleyball Fun

Introduce volleyball to little hands with the bump and pass of a beach ball — it's lighter and larger and enables kids to achieve almost immediate success in controlling direction and distance without the frustration of the heavier regulation ball. After teaching kids the object of the game and rules for rotation, use the beach ball as the game ball. There's no need for serves at this point — one team just puts the ball in play.

MICHAEL WILSON

Let Yourself Go

Shake off restlessness by having students stand up and exercise to the words of this classroom movement activity:

Let your hands
Go pop, pop, pop.
Let your arms
Go flop, flop, flop.
Let your head
Bob in and out.
Let your shoulders
Move about.
Let your thumbs
Move side to side.
Let your knees
Move way out wide.
Let your eyebrows
Wiggle, wiggle.
Let your body
Jiggle, jiggle.
Let yourself go
Any way on
This
Pop, flop,
in and out,
move about,
side to side,
way out wide,
wiggle, jiggle,
let-yourself-go day.

CAROL QUINN

Physical Education

Wheel Of Exercise

The Wheel of Exercise is a good way to liven up an indoor physical education class.

To make the wheel, cut a large circle from poster board. Divide it into six or eight sections and label each with a specific exercise such as "jumping jacks" or "run in place." Mount the circle on a large square of cardboard with a paper fastener. Make it loose so it will spin easily. Draw an arrow on the cardboard pointing to the circle.

To choose the first exercise of the day, have one student spin the wheel and then lead the class in the designated exercise. The end result? No more groans at the thought of basic exercises.

LORRIE JONES

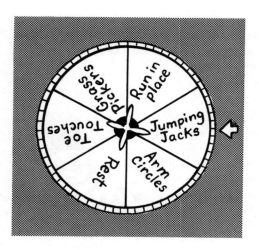

Free Program

To receive the Amateur Athletic Union's free program guide to physical fitness, write Physical Fitness Program, 160 HPER Bldg., Bloomington, IN 47405. Teachers with handicapped students may call the AAU, collect, at (812) 335-2059, for ideas on how to modify exercises.

JUDITH GASTON FISHER

Super Scoops

Looking for an inexpensive addition to your P.E. or playground equipment? Recycle gallon plastic milk bottles into super scoops kids can use for toss-and-catch games.

Ask kids to bring in clean, empty plastic bottles. Use a utility knife to cut off the top and neck of each bottle, leaving the handle and lower half to form the scoop.

Kids use the scoops in pairs to play catch or alone to bounce a ball on the floor and catch it. Or, place the class about 20 feet from a wall and ask them to throw a ball against the wall and scoop it on the bounce. Younger children can sit on the floor and roll a ball into a partner's scoop.

These super scoops store easily — just stack one inside the other. JAYNE HUEBNER

For Third Graders And Up

Whether you're in charge of physical education or whether you have occasional recess duty, give children plenty of time to practice physical skills. For instance, before asking students to play softball, give them time to practice batting, throwing, and catching. Award skill certificates when a child can throw the softball 30 feet to another player with accuracy; catch a softball three out of five times from a distance of 20 feet or more; or bat a properly pitched softball five out of 10 times.

Just as you wouldn't teach math skills with one pencil for everyone, so you shouldn't teach physical skills with only one ball! If you're short on standard equipment, ask parents to donate such recyclables as old tennis balls. Put them in the dryer for a little extra oomph. Practice soccer skills with empty plastic milk jugs.

ARTIE KAMIYA

Fitness

Fitness For Everyone

The early Greeks described the special relationship between fitness and the body with what we call calisthenics. Kallos means the action of building beauty and sthenos is increasing strength through exercise. Create this beautiful strength in your students by using the cardiovascular fitness activities described here. You and your students will become healthier and happier!

Follow the Fitness Leader

Divide your class into groups of six to eight students. Each group stands in a circle 10 feet in diameter. Select one student to be the Fitness Leader for each group. Each leader stands in the center of the group's circle. Play an upbeat song on a record player or cassette player as the Fitness Leaders lead their groups in exercise. For example, if the Fitness Leader does jumping jacks, then the rest of the students follow suit. On your command of "New Fitness Leader," the student in the center of each group points to a new student who then goes to the center of the circle to be the new leader. Continue the activity until all of the students get to be the Fitness Leader during a three-to-four-minute song. You can vary this activity by adding commands such as "All jog in place," "All skip clockwise," or "Pushup power!...do three pushups."

Fitness Square Dance

Here's a novel way to introduce students to a few of the basic square dance skills. Select several players to be "It," who will try to tag the other students. Once tagged, students must "freeze," but may be "unfrozen" by performing a series of square dance moves, such as a "do-si-do" or "right elbow swing," with other frozen students. Put on some toe-tapping bluegrass music and you're ready to go!

Jumpnastics Workout

Want to challenge your students? Record about 30 seconds each of five or six popular songs on a cassette, leaving roughly 20 seconds of "dead" time between songs. When the music plays, your entire class can either jog in place or perform an activity you lead. When the music stops, give a certain exercise for your students to do, such as five pushups. When the music starts again, continue doing a slow jog, jumping in place, or new exercises like arm circles or general stretching.

Taking Things To Heart

Introduce this activity, which integrates math with health and fitness concepts, by saying, "Did you know that your heart is a muscle? In fact, it is the only hollow muscle in your body. Like all the other muscles in your body, your heart stays strong when it exercises. Let's see how exercise makes your heart work and keep strong."

Students graph their heart rates while engaged in different activities. Start off with students sitting at their desks to find their pulses either at the radial artery (at the wrist, near the base of the thumb) or carotid artery (on either side of the neck). They should gently press their forefingers at either of these two sites and count for a 15-second period, then multiply their results by four to get the beats-per-minute. Next, students perform a number of different activities, such as jogging in place, doing jumping jacks, etc., recording their heart rates during each activity and graphing the results.

Lead a discussion about what happens to the heart rate during more vigorous activities. Explain that blood is really a special "conveyor belt" that brings oxygen to the muscles and carries off unwanted by-products produced by the muscles. Also, talk about the many benefits of exercise and use the handy reproducible at the right to enhance your unit.

ARTIE KAMIYA

Fitness

Minutes For Muscles

Take a few minutes each day to introduce your students to the scientific names of their muscles and bones. The "Bone of the Week" or "Muscles of the Month" can be reinforced by playing the following games:

Everyone's heard of the game Simon Says. But here's a game with a twist! In Dr. Simon Says, you or an appointed leader call out the scientific names of different body parts. Students follow directions as in a game of Simon Says, except no student is eliminated from the game (because Dr. Simon says: "For greater student participation....eliminate elimination!")

Use the following sample bone recognition commands as you play this game: "touch your mandible" (jaw), "touch your cranium (head) five times," "rub your patella" (kneecap), "scratch your scapula" (back of shoulder), or "beat your sternum" (chest).

Here's another way to help your students remember important facts about their bodies. Just take a sheet of 8 1/2-by 11-inch construction paper or tagboard and cut it into eight rectangles. On four of the rectangles, write the scientific name of the bone or muscle. On the other four, write their common names. For example, "stomach muscles" and "abdominals," or "hip or pelvic bone" and "ilium." Let your students match up the scientific names with the more common names.

ARTIE KAMIYA

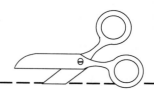

Benefits of exercise worksheet

Finish the phrases with the words given at right.

Exercise...

1. gives you more _____
2. improves your self-_____
3. tones your _____
4. helps you feel _____
5. helps you fall _____
6. helps you cope with _____
7. helps you lose _____
8. increases your resistance to _____
9. counters anxiety and _____
10. makes your heart _____
11. provides a way to share activities with _____

relaxed
friends
stress
fatigue
muscles
stronger
depression
asleep
energy
weight
image

Nutrition/Dental Health

Tic-Tac-Toe To Health!

Students paste pictures of nutritious foods onto large" O's", junk foods onto large "X's." Laminate, play, and cheer for good health.
NANCY PANOS

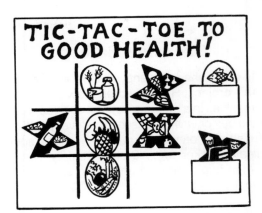

Parent/Student Breakfast

Reinforce with your class the importance of eating a nutritious breakfast. Once a month before classes begin, hold a parent/student breakfast. Ask parents to provide utensils and food for themselves and their child. Have milk available for purchase.

This activity is also a great way for everyone to get to know each other.
MARY DAUBERSMITH

Nutrition And Teeth

Do not ignore the place of nutrition when discussing the steps to healthy teeth and gums. Calcium, phosphorus, and fluorine are three minerals necessary for good teeth. Vitamin C is important for healthy gums.

Research with the class those foods that are rich in calcium — milk, greens (especially spinach and kale), broccoli, oranges, and so on. Remind pupils that milk, the most important source of calcium, can come in many forms, from cheese to ice cream to cream soups and puddings. Create a large chart on which you keep track of how many servings of these foods class members eat in two or three days. Count total class servings rather than individual ones so that pupils whose families do not serve these foods will not be embarrassed.

Do the same activity with phosphorus and Vitamin C. Foods rich in phosphorus include meat, fish, cereal products, eggs, and milk. Good vitamin C foods are oranges and other citrus fruits, papaya, broccoli, brussels sprouts, cabbage, spinach, kale, tomatoes, berries.

After two or three days, total the class servings for each mineral and vitamin and divide to find an average per pupil.

Although fluorine is available in such foods as fish and dry beans, the best source of this mineral is water. Suggest the class consult someone responsible for the local water supply to see how much fluorine there is in the water. Is it adequate? Is stannous fluoride added? Why? Why not?

Finally, create a class report on the findings, along with conclusions and recommendations about any changes that should be made in eating habits. Send copies home for parent reading.

Body Awareness/Safety

Exercise Safety

To easily show students how fog limits visibility, try this project. Have children draw a picture of themselves in a morning setting, such as waiting for the bus or walking to school. Cover the picture with sheets of waxed paper — more sheets indicate thicker fog. Discuss safety tips like wearing bright clothing and using extra caution on foggy days.
DIANNE LADD

Is There A Doctor In The Class?

Try this idea to reinforce learning about body systems and their parts for a science or health lesson. Divide the class into five groups. Put each group in charge of a different body system: the circulatory, respiratory, skeletal, muscular and digestive system.

One child in each group lies on a large piece of butcher paper while another child traces the outline of the prone child's body. The students then draw and label the body parts on the paper for their assigned system.

Pretend the students are doctors who are attending an important medical convention and are specialists in their fields. The children are assigned different roles in their individual groups, such as doctor in charge, medical researcher, materials technician and reporter. When students have finished their projects, they share their work with the rest of the class and present their medical "findings" as a team of doctors would.

The finished drawings make an interesting bulletin board or hall display.
CHERYL KELLER

Modern Medicine

Help students appreciate the great advances that have been made in the field of medicine over the years. Begin a class scrapbook of newspaper and magazine clippings and spend a few minutes each day discussing one of the items. Then group the clippings into categories such as: new medicines and medical equipment, organ transplants, discovery of new diseases, preventive medicine, world health problems, and so on. Add new items as they are found.

Ask pupils to talk to older relatives or friends about some of today's medical practices that were unknown to most people when they were children. For example, an organ transplant is rather common today, but the idea would have been beyond the wildest imagination of most people during the childhood of pupils' great grandparents.

Immunization Chart

Create a chart listing all the vaccinations and inoculations that are required by your school or state. Opposite each item, leave room for a date to be added. At the top of the page, write "Immunization Record for _____." Leave room for pupils to add a decorative border or other illustrations. Duplicate the chart.

Discuss with pupils the importance of having these immunizations and then send home as many copies as there are children in the family. Suggest parents insert the correct dates and use the charts to record the date each child received the appropriate immunization.

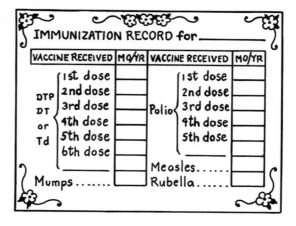

7 Art, Music, and Creative Dramatics

Introduction

Art, music and creative dramatics — subjects so valuable for a well-rounded person, yet so often neglected in our concern for teaching the basics. Do not let that happen in your classroom. Use the ideas here to help pupils appreciate music, find joy in painting an art "masterpiece," experience a thrill in interpreting a concept through creative movement.

Color Search

Give kids an art lesson on the variety within primary and secondary colors, then send them on a scavenger hunt — right at their desks. Assign each child a color and ask him or her to search through magazines to cut out examples of that color. Then ask kids to paste all of their samples on a large piece of construction paper. Students can compare the variety of shades and tones and give each shade an original, descriptive name.   MARY MATTHEWS

Jump-Start Art

If you're tired of hearing, "I don't know what to draw," relax. Here's a simple way to motivate students. Bring in a box filled with small fabric scraps, string, yarn, buttons, etc. Let students select one item from the box and glue it to a sheet of colorful paper. They can draw, paint, color or use markers.   HELEN WUBBENHORST

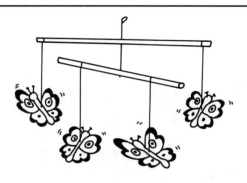

Monarch Mobile

Combine art and science in a study of the monarch butterfly. Students use library books and encyclopedias to research size, coloration, and design. Next, children draw two identical butterflies on paper, including details and using the correct colors. Kids cut out butterflies and glue back-to-back, then attach to a cotton swab body. String butterflies together to form a mobile or place on a colorful spring bulletin board.
FRED PHILLIPS

Sun Fades

Demonstrate the powerful effect of the sun with this project that combines science and art. Give each child a piece of manila paper. Ask him or her to draw and cut out a shape — butterfly, flower, kite. Then staple this cutout to a piece of colored construction paper. Tape these to a window with the shapes facing the sunlight. After two weeks, take down the papers and remove staples. The sun will have faded the paper all around the cutouts, but the papers underneath will retain their original colors. Combine these sun-fade images to make an unusual bulletin board display.
BETTIE WALKER

Kitchen Prints

Here's a fun art project for primary children using ordinary kitchen utensils. Have children dip a variety of kitchen utensils into containers of red, blue, and yellow tempera paint (one utensil per color) and then print random designs on construction paper. Jar lids, potato mashers, and forks are good objects to use. The outcome is a pattern of overlapping colors and designs.
MARDI GORK

Mystery Message Mural

Here's a nifty mural for your class to make this spring. On a large sheet of butcher paper, pencil the word "Spring" in big letters. Then cut the paper into as many sections as there are students, making sure that each piece contains a part of a letter. Now have students use the papers to draw pictures of things that represent spring. Make sure students understand that they should draw right over the pencil markings. They should then outline their completed pictures in red and trace the pencil markings in black.

Finally, have students piece together their papers to form a mural and discover the message. This idea can work for any subject or season.
JULIE STEMPINSKI

Student Art Teachers

Provide students with an opportunity to discover new art activities, share ideas, and give directions. Ask for volunteers to introduce an art project to the class. These students use library books or craft magazines to find projects, or come up with their own ideas. Ask each volunteer to prepare a materials list, written directions, and sample project for you to review. Then schedule time each week for a student art teacher with an approved project to teach a craft lesson. LINDA MARTIN MERCER

Class Mobile

A mobile can be more than just a classroom decoration — it can serve as a unique class self-portrait. Ask students to identify their likes or dislikes. Then have each student draw him or herself engaged in a favorite activity. Cut the figure out and punch a hole through the top. Suspend the illustrated figures from pieces of string attached to rods in interesting clusters. Hang the finished product in a central location for all to see and enjoy.
DIANE UDELL

New Twist To Problem Solving

To encourage critical thinking skills, try this creative group art project. Divide the class into groups of three or four. Give each group a bag that contains two large sheets of construction paper, one bottle of glue, one package of markers, five scraps of colored tissue paper, two brads (or paper fasteners), one yard of yarn, scissors, and an index card. Have each group use the items to make and decorate a particular object, such as a three-dimensional tree. Give them one hour (or less) to complete the project. Groups should use their index cards to name the project and list the names of group members.

For a variation, use different supplies to let groups create airplanes that fly, mobiles that balance, monsters that stand, and so on.
MIDGE PIPPEL

String Impressions

Students get a good feel for texture while working with thin paper and string, or rickrack. Place the string or rickrack on the table or desk and let it snake around or overlap itself. Tell the students to make a design with the string. Then put the thin paper over that. Use the flat side of the crayon and shade over the string or use short strokes with the point of the crayon for variation. Children may use a variety of colors or concentrate on a more monochromatic theme. The results are "impressive."
HELEN WUBBENHORST

Soap Paints

Take your class outside on a sunny day to enjoy this art activity. Make your own finger paints by mixing three cups of powdered laundry detergent and one cup of water. Use less detergent if you're painting with brushes. When the desired consistency is achieved, kids add food coloring — one drop at a time — to create pastel colors. Cleanup is a breeze.
JOAN SCHORNSTAED

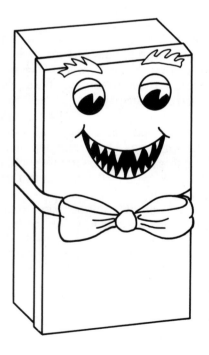

Crayon Monster

Make a crayon monster using tape, a shoe box, construction paper and paints. Tape the shoe box lid onto the shoe box. Stand the shoe box on end vertically. Cut a hole in the top end of the box for a mouth. Paint or glue on construction paper features to the box to make it look like a friendly monster. Glue construction paper teeth around the cut-out mouth area.

Introduce the crayon monster to your class. Students should peel the paper wrapping off of their small or broken crayons, discard the paper and put the crayons into the monster's mouth.

At the end of the year, the monster pays the children back for being so kind to him. Remove the crayons that have collected in the box. Line a cupcake tin with cupcake liners. Fill each liner halfway with various stubs of paperless crayons. Bake them at 350 degrees Fahrenheit for five minutes, or until crayons melt.

Let the crayon cakes cool for 30 minutes and harden. After they have hardened, peel off liner paper. You will have a multi-colored crayon cake. Give each child a large piece of art paper and a crayon cake. They will enjoy creating pictures with their crazy crayon cakes.
MARY DINNEEN

Music

Class Flag

A class flag can create a sense of unity. Make a simple design using black marker on an old pillow case or sheet. Cut the material into small squares, one per child. Distribute the squares and ask them to color in the design with markers.

Have students assemble the flag with scotch tape. Sew or laminate the finished flag together and attach it to a dowel rod for display. You can even write a special class pledge.

GUINN VANZANT

Water Gun Mural

Plan this outdoor painting activity carefully, then stand back as kids use squirt guns to create a colorful mural. First, tape plenty of newspaper to a wall or fence to shield from paint. Next, tape a large piece of white butcher paper over the newspaper. Using only primary colors — red, yellow, blue — mix tempera paints with water to achieve a thin consistency, then pour each color into a separate water gun. Give kids three tries with each color gun. Children demonstrate the effect of mixing colors as they create this class masterpiece of modern art.

TERI HARRISON

Finger Paint A Rainbow

A finger painting experience is a fun way to introduce the color wheel to students. Begin the lesson by asking students what three colors are primary colors. Explain that primary colors are those that cannot be made by combining any other colors, and all colors except black and white are made from primary colors.

When students discover that red, yellow and blue are primary colors, give each child two pieces of finger paint paper or construction paper. One piece is used for mixing the paint; the other is used for painting or drawing.

Place a tablespoon of each of the primary colors on each student's paper. Ask students to experiment with the three colors and make their own secondary colors, such as purple, orange and green. Suggest to the students that they use the colors to make a rainbow design or picture. Warn students that if they mix all three colors together they will get brown.

Be prepared to see a number of beautiful rainbows!

BEVERLY J. ANDERSON

Music Mania

To put some variety into your music program, try these ideas that boost thinking skills. Suggest that students:
• Design a new cover for a favorite album.
• Listen to an instrumental record and list the instruments they hear.
• Find a unique way to display the names of this week's top ten recordings. For example, make a wall chart or a pyramid-shaped poster.
• Listen to ten or more songs. Classify their titles under such headings as rock, jazz, folk, country, and classical.
• Conduct a survey to find out which radio stations classmates, teachers, parents, and friends listen to. Graph the information and then make conclusions based on the data.
• Draw a cartoon strip based on the lyrics of a song.

PAULA MACDONALD

Music Man

Use poster board to make different musical symbols for Music Man's body. Help students learn music fundamentals by labeling the parts of his body on plain white note cards. Students select a note card from a pocket attached to the board and place the label next to the correct musical symbol. Head the creation "Taking Note of Music Fundamentals."

VERENA L. CHANCE

Music

Rhythmic Activities

Hand out rhythm instruments, and ask kids to experiment — one at a time to keep noise under control — with the sounds their instruments make. Then, together, tell a story using the instruments. Ask students to name sounds heard in a zoo, for example — elephants trumpeting, birds singing, lions roaring, buffalo stomping. Which instruments bring to mind those sounds? What would the zoo sound like at night? If you got locked in, would you be afraid? Excited? Which instruments could help express your feelings? Write the story as a class, then ask one child to narrate it while the others play on cue.

Use the instruments to introduce students to basic concepts of rhythm. Chant this rhythm with the class:

*Clap, Clap, *Clap-pi-ty *Clap*
*Clap-pi-ty *Clap-pi-ty *Clap, Clap*

Repeat the rhythm, clapping only on the italicized syllables for the pulse. Follow with claps on the syllables with asterisks for the accent rhythm.

Last, clap on every syllable to hear the word rhythm.

Now classify the instruments — by high, medium, and heavy sounds or by those that are struck, plucked, blown into, or shaken. Use instruments with heavy sounds to play the accents, medium sounds for the pulse, and high sounds for the word rhythm. While you continue reciting the chant, ask one group at a time to play, then add the others. It will challenge kids to hear several rhythms going simultaneously, so keep it simple for primaries.

Make the activity more interesting by adding words to the chant, using the same rhythm:

*Now hear *ev'-ry-one *play*
(Everyone plays.)
*Now the *mu-sic is *soft*
(Everyone plays softer.)

Create different effects by changing the word *soft* to *loud*, *fast*, or *slow* and by assigning instruments to be played at different times.

ELVA DANIELS

Creating Some

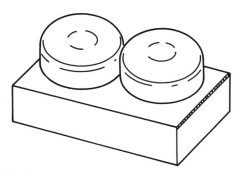

Bongos
Cut off the bottom sections of two plastic bleach bottles and discard the rest. Cut holes the same size as the bottle pieces in the bottom of a shallow cardboard box. Flip the box upside down, insert the bottles, and fasten to the inside of the box with masking tape.

ELVA DANIELS

Tambourine
This may not look like a traditional tambourine, but it sounds similar. Start with a wooden dowel or part of a discarded broom handle. Loosely nail bottle caps to the handle. Shake or twist from side to side for a jingle-jangle sound.

ELVA DANIELS

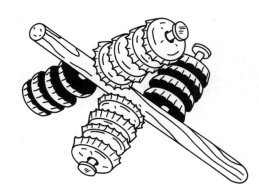

Rhythm Instruments

Garden Hose Trumpet

Cut a 1-foot section from a discarded garden hose. Tape a kitchen funnel to the severed end. Blow into the faucet connection to create a bugle sound. ELVA DANIELS

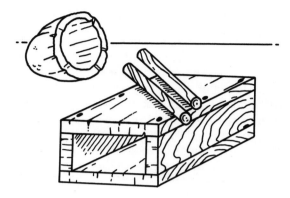

Temple Blocks

Make an oblong box out of hardwood, and leave the ends open. Strike the box with a coconut shell or a hardwood stick. EDWIN PETERS

Pipe Bells

Nail together a wooden frame. Cut an electrical or water pipe into graduated lengths. Suspend the pipes on the frame, in order of length, by pulling a piece of wire through each pipe, then winding the ends around nails driven into both sides. A simpler way to create a bell sound is to fill four or five glasses of the same size with different amounts of water. To play the pipes or glasses, tap with a stick. EDWIN PETERS

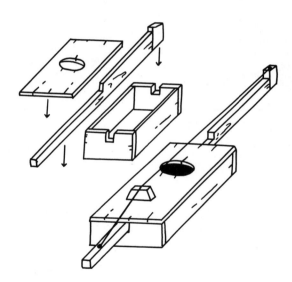

Upright Bass

Cut a hole in the lid of a small, sturdy box. Notch the shorter sides of the box, then insert a fingerboard, made from tightly-rolled construction paper or wood cut as shown, in the notches. Attach the box lid. Glue a cardboard or wooden bridge in the shape of a truncated triangle onto the lid, several inches below the hole. Attach thin nylon string to the top and bottom of the fingerboard so that the line is taut and rests on the bridge. Pluck the string, pressing and moving fingers up and down its length to vary the pitch. ELVA DANIELS

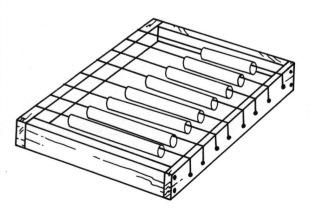

Rhythm Instruments

Snare Drum

Remove the lid from an empty cookie tin and save to use in making the cymbal. Turn the cookie tin upside down and place about 20 paper clips in the recessed bottom. Cut a piece of cardboard the same diameter as the tin. Place it over — not into — the bottom and secure with masking tape. Use chopsticks or pencils to play.
EDWIN PETERS

Washtub or Box Bass

Make a tiny hole in the center of the bottom of an old plastic washtub or a wooden crate. Tie an old key to one end of a piece of twine or nylon. Pull the line through the hole so that the key secures it inside the container. Attach the other end to the top of an old broom handle. Let the bottom of the handle remain free so that the line can be pulled taut. Play by plucking.
EDWIN PETERS

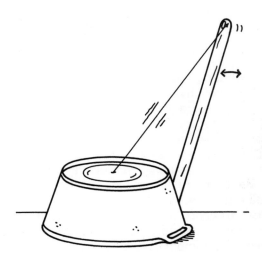

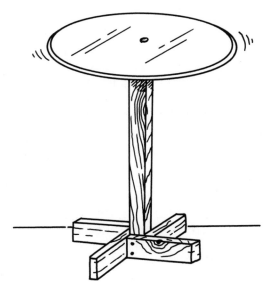

Cymbal

Nail together four pieces of sturdy wood to form a base. Attach a vertical piece to the base to make a stand. Loosely nail a flat pan lid or a cookie-tin lid to the stand. The lid must be able to vibrate when struck by a chopstick or pencil.
EDWIN PETERS

Music

Music Across the Curriculum

Use music to enhance your curriculum and give your class something to sing about.

Musical Language Arts!

• You've got rhythm and so do many names, words, and sounds. Ask students to listen for rhythmic patterns created in speech, by equipment, in nature. Discuss the patterns they find. Suggest that students use cassette recorders to record rhythmic patterns they hear outside or at home. Ask kids to bring their tapes to school for a rhythm sharing session.

• Are chants popular with your students? Rhythm is an important part of cheers and even jumprope jingles. Try composing your own class chant.

• Discuss rhythm in literature and poetry. In the story UMBRELLA, by Tara Yashima (Penguin, 1977), the rhythmic structure of the words helps the reader hear the rain falling on a new umbrella. Can students find other books where rhythmic words enhance the story line? What about a favorite poem? Practice reading the words aloud accompanied by rhythm instruments, then perform for another class.

• Music can enhance creative writing, too. Offer children an example by listening to a recording of PETER AND THE WOLF, by Sergei Prokofiev. Help kids recognize the musical themes that identify each character. Then suggest that children work in small groups to write their own stories. Tape musical themes that represent their main characters, and perform stories aloud accompanied by the taped music.

• Singing is a great opportunity for oral expression. WE ALL LIVE TOGETHER, a four-volume series distributed by Youngheart Records, is excellent for sing-alongs.

Social Studies In Scale

• Lyrics can teach, too. For example, folksongs may offer insights and information about historical events or reminders about our cultural heritage. Ballads may tell stories based on true incidents or characters. Ask kids to analyze songs for historical information, then to check for accuracy. Or try writing a ballad together about a historical or current event.

Classical Science

• Ask your librarian or music specialist to help you find musical selections that illustrate a topic in science. For instance, broaden a unit on weather by listening to musical interpretations of a storm. You might compare "The Storm" from Gioacchino Rossini's WILLIAM TELL OVERTURE, Ferde Grofe's GRAND CANYON SUITE, and Ludwig van Beethoven's PASTORAL SYMPHONY. What kind of mood did each composer create? How are the elements — lightning, thunder, rain — created? Older kids might enjoy listening to recordings at the library to find selections for future units.

There's Math In Music?

• It may be only simple counting, but for a musician, counting beats is critical when composing music or when playing it. Invite a music teacher to talk to your class about musical notation and how the notes determine the number of beats in each measure. Look at simple sheet music together and count the beats. Discuss how a small difference in the number of beats can create the difference between a waltz (3/4 time) and a march (4/4 time).

MARDI GORK

Creative Dramatics

Act-ivities

Help children acquire concepts and skills through creative dramatics.

Science

Have younger students act out the growth of a seedling from seed to adult plant; different children may represent the seed, the soil, the rain, wind or sun.

For older children, students can become parts of the solar system, demonstrating the rotation and revolution of planets and moons around the sun. Students can also represent the neutrons, protons, and electrons in an atom (show positive charges with smiles and negative ones with frowns). Completed rings and "bonding" can be shown with the linking of arms.

Language Arts

Teach subjects and predicates by having one student represent the subject (or actor). He or she is unable to move until the student chosen as the verb tells him or her what to do. When the verb "arrives" and tells the subject to "jump," both may show the action. This method can also be used to show whether sentences are complete or sentence fragments.

Older children can act out the three kinds of verbs; verbs showing action, auxiliary verbs working together to "help" the action verbs, and linking verbs (connect the student subject to the student's complement by having them link arms). Try this format to show compound subjects, verbs, and sentences.

Social Studies

Try reenacting events from history, with your students improvising dialogue according to how they believe the character would have responded in the situation. Place different historical characters in situations they were not actually involved in to determine how history might have been different. Children can also research the actual event and portray what actually happened as clearly as they can.   HOLLEE A. FRICK

8 Across the Curriculum

Introduction

How do you capitalize on class interest in the latest space probe or a general interest in birds, winter, or sports? By integrating cross-curriculum activities. Such a simple thing as an apple, for example, can inspire math, science, art and language activities. Read and use many of the ideas in this chapter, adapt others to fit the topics you and your class are talking about.

What A Character!

Here's a cross-curricular activity that combines creative writing, social studies, and art. As part of a lesson on character description, have students choose a secret character from history or current events to describe in detail. Then, after they've completed their character sketches, have them create masks to represent their chosen characters. Students can then tape their character descriptions onto the backs of the masks. As a final exercise, ask each student to present his or her character sketch and mask to the class, and have students guess who the secret character is. After everyone has taken a turn, display the masks on the bulletin board.   PAMELA ANN LEONARD

Classifying Crayons

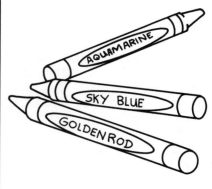

What can you do with a box of crayons? Besides coloring, my class enjoys these classifying activities.

Identify crayons with names containing compound words, such as goldenrod, cornflower, aquamarine, and bittersweet.

Find crayons with names that contain adjectives to describe the crayon's color, such as brick red, sky blue, midnight blue, carnation pink, forest green, olive green, and so on.

Make lists of crayons that belong together in a certain group. For example, greens, blues, reds; warm/cool; light/dark, or other classifications. Afterwards, have children graph the results.

JULIE S. POLAK

Thematic Unit — Apples

A Juicy Lesson With Apples

This curriculum-based lesson is sure to be the apple of the class' eye!

Critical Thinking

Show the class a red apple and a ripe tomato. Challenge the class with a comment such as: "I have two apples in my hand. Would you like to eat them?"

When children tell you that you really have a tomato and an apple, ask them to prove it.

When they reason that "the apple is red," you say, "So is the tomato." Continue challenging students as they try to prove you have a tomato and an apple.

After discussing the physical qualities of apples, ask children to draw a vertical line down the center of a piece of paper. On the left half of the paper have students print "The Same" and on the right half, "Different." Ask students to list similarities and differences between apples and tomatoes. Similarities can be: Both are red and have skin and seeds. Differences can include: Apple skin is tougher, the apple is a member of the rose family, and seeds are different in size, shape and color. Continue the discussion with the story of Johnny Appleseed — the man who brought apple trees to the Ohio Valley and Indiana. Ask students about their favorite types of apples and the various ways apples are used. Read and discuss poetry and prose about apples, apple folklore and legends, etc. If time permits, plan a visit to an orchard or a cider mill.

Poetry

Ask children to write a poem about apples or apple-related subjects. Bobbing for apples, a worm in an apple, apple blossoms in springtime, Johnny Appleseed or climbing the old apple tree are some possible topics. Here is a sample poem to read to the class:

A Good Friend
High up in the tree
A lovely apple grew
Shiny red, it blushed at me
And said, "I'm here for you!"

Math

Children can practice measurement skills by making applesauce with careful teacher supervision. For about 20 students you will need:
• 12 to 15 medium to large apples with bright red skins for colorful applesauce

• child safety knives (such as the Pumpkin Kutter, sold at drugstores and discount stores)
• electric frying pan with lid — to be operated by teacher only
• wooden spoon
• 1/2 cup or more of white sugar (amount varies with tartness of apples and personal taste)
• large sieve
• paper cups, plastic spoons

Directions:

1. Students cut apples in half, then quarters. If apples are large, cut in eighths. Compare fraction sizes and discuss differences.
2. Teacher adds enough water to frying pan to cover bottom.
3. Students add apples to pan. Teacher covers pan and simmers apples at medium temperature until they are "slushy." Teacher stirs often to keep apples from sticking or burning.
4. Discuss new vocabulary words: steam, simmer, boil, pulp, etc.
5. Let apples cool. Students strain cooked, soft apples through coarse sieve into large bowl. Use back of wooden spoon to force apple pulp through sieve.

Measure 1/8 cup of sugar first, then 1/4 cup, noting the mathematical quantities. Students add sugar to taste, and stir to dissolve. When using the word dissolve, ask children to explain what it means.

6. Ask students to divide the applesauce. Ask how many paper cups are needed. How many spoons? If they know how many paper cups are needed, will the number of spoons be the same or different? Why or why not?
7. Enjoy!

Art

Make apple mobiles using construction paper, yarn and glue. Cut two top and two bottom pieces from red or green paper for apples. Cut two center pieces from white paper to resemble core. Draw seeds on core with black crayon or marker. Lay a long piece of yarn on back of apple pieces. Make sure pieces don't touch each other. Staple or glue yarn onto back of each piece. Then staple or glue back piece of each section to front piece, back to back. Hang from a window or ceiling to display.

MARY F. MACDONALD

Thematic Unit — Birds

Birds, Birds, Birds

These activities will arouse children's interest in birds and, at the same time, enhance skills in math, reading, writing, art and creative thinking.

Math

Lead a discussion on the energy needs of birds. Birds, like most other small, active animals burn up a lot of fuel. Baby birds, because of their rapid growth and high metabolism, consume so much food that if human babies were to eat as much for their size, they would soon look like blimps! Many baby birds and some adults — hummingbirds, for instance — eat twice their own weight in food in a day. Let's hope no one in your class "eats like a bird!"

Have students figure out how many pounds of food they would have to eat in a day to "eat like a baby bird." Students multiply their individual weight by two. Next, they convert the number of pounds into specific food items. For example, if a typical hamburger weighs one-quarter pound, how many hamburgers would they have to consume per day? Bowls of ice cream? Peanut butter sandwiches? Loaves of bread?

Put a scale in the classroom and let children weigh their lunches, then figure out how many lunches of the same size they would have to eat every day to roughly equal, for their size, the amount baby birds eat for their size.

Science/Research

Discuss different types of beaks that the kids have noticed. Ask, "What do they look like and how are they used? Has anyone seen how a cardinal opens a sunflower seed?" (Crunches the shell with its fat, strong seed-cracker bill.) "How about a chickadee" (Holds the seed with one foot and pecks at it with its short, sharp beak.) "What about other species you have seen? Parakeets? Canaries? Parrots?"

The class can keep a record for a week of how various birds use their beaks. A bird guide in the classroom will help the kids identify the birds they see, but they could write descriptions and draw pictures instead.

Alternatively, each child could do some library research and write a report on one or more different types of beaks — their shapes and how they are used. To be sure that a wide variety will

be represented, you might have the children choose from a list (such as spoonbill, woodcock, mallard duck, nuthatch, chickadee, goldfinch, pelican, loon, crow, jay, skimmer, hawk, owl, pigeon, starling, sparrow, blackbird, oriole, warbler, woodpecker, crossbill, heron and parrot, to name a few.)

At the end of the week, have the children present informal reports to the class.

Science

Discuss different types of habitats with the class (forest, brushy area, meadow, marsh, city park, farm, suburban yard, tropical rain forest, desert, arctic tundra, ocean and sandy beach). Ask, "Might some birds be found in several different habitats?" (Certainly!) "Might a bird feed in a different habitat from where it nests?" (Yes.)

Let students research various local birds with emphasis on where the birds are most likely to be found. Three-dimensional habitat miniatures are fun and educational to make, using shoe (or other small) boxes placed on their sides. Students add colorful pictures of birds to the scenes. Plan this activity for winter or spring when there are plenty of dried plants to use for some of the materials.

Science

Lead a discussion about the types of nests birds make. (Mud bowls lined with plants; plant or animal materials woven into bags or cups; lined cavities in trees; burrows dug in soft cliffs or the ground; saliva nests made by certain swiftlets, then put into bird's nest soup by humans; and floating mounds of vegetation.) Ask, "How do birds know how to make their nests?" (Inborn ability which, however, improves with experience.) "How do humans know how to make their homes?" (Learned or figured out.) "Is a bird nest really like a human home?" (Humans live in homes their entire lives. Most birds use their nests only to raise their young; as soon as the young have fledged, the nest is abandoned. So a nest is really more like a cradle.)

Take the class to an area with a good supply of mud and grass and let students make their own nests. Even with our advanced brains and agile fingers, making a nest is not so easy!

ELIZABETH D. DARLINGTON

Science/Math

Connecting Science And Math

By combining the teaching of math and science — whether it's graphing or estimating, measurement or statistics, geometry or logic — your students will learn that math lays a solid foundation for the study of science. Here are a few suggestions to get you started.

Plant Patterns

Let's say your science text has a unit on plants, and you bring in leaves for students to look at, perhaps to identify with a field guide. Make the lesson do double duty by using the leaves to teach sets.

Have students arrange the leaves in three groups: leaves with sharp edges, leaves with rounded edges, and leaves with smooth edges. Give the students string loops. Ask them to put a large loop around all the leaves and smaller loops around each of the three kinds of leaves. Have them label each loop: LEAVES, sharp-edged, round-edged, smooth-edged.

The Vastness of Space

Your class is ready to tackle a unit on the solar system. The text is full of pictures, diagrams and charts of the planets, giving the size of each and its distance from the sun. These may be the first really large numbers your students have encountered.

The maximum distance from the sun for the following planets is: Mercury — 69,700,000 kilometers (km); Venus — 109,000,000 km; Earth — 152,000,000 km. Explain that because these numbers are so large, scientists and mathematicians use a shorthand to write them. Show students how to express the distances in scientific notation. For example, 69,700,000 km $= 6.97 \times 10^7$ km and 109,000,000 km $= 1.09 \times 10^8$ km.

Extend that activity by having students think of other numbers that would be easier to express in scientific notation. Some examples: world populations, the time it takes a planet like Uranus to orbit the sun, or the age of the Earth.

Earth Algebra

Earth Science is the unit heading, and you plan to teach students about the globe. When you describe longitude and latitude, you are introducing the idea of coordinates. Build on this by having students create maps of local interest — your classroom, the path they take to get to school each day, or your town. Have students draw their maps on graph paper and label them with coordinate numbers and letters. Show the class how to create an index for the map giving the coordinates of various landmarks.

Even young students will like this introduction to coordinates, a concept that prepares them for algebra.

Living Fractions

You are working on the plant reproduction chapter in your text and will have the students grow plants from seeds. Here's an opportunity to introduce fractions into the science activity. Have each student count the number of seeds that were planted. After a few days, have students count the number of seeds that actually sprouted. Show the class how to write a fraction that describes the part of the planted seeds that sprouted:

- number of sprouts
- number of seeds planted

Explain that this fraction, called the germination rate, is an important number for farmers and others who grow plants for a living. It helps them decide how many seeds to plant in order to get the number of plants they need.

Put each student's name and germination rate on the board. Ask the class to identify the largest and smallest fraction. Have students estimate the average or help older students calculate it.

Another logical math activity would be to have students measure the height of each seedling at intervals and graph the growth of the plants.

LAUREL GALBRAITH SHERMAN

Thematic Unit—the Ocean

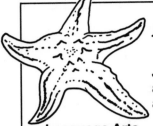

All Aboard For An Oceanography Lesson

Ahoy, matey! Introduce students to oceanography and marine biology by reading Jules Verne's classic, 20,000 LEAGUES UNDER THE SEA Then set sail for adventure as your class becomes an oceanarium with these across-the-curriculum activities!

Language Arts

Launch a language arts lesson with peri-graphs (periscope-shaped poems) comparing the sea and land. A peri-graph starts with a subject at the top and switches to a different, and sometimes opposite, subject at the bottom. Follow this guide when writing a peri-graph:

1. Select a noun and place on line 1. (subject a)
2. Write two adjectives describing subject a and place on line 2.
3. Write three participles (the noun form of verbs ending in "ing") describing subject a. Place on line 3.
4. Select another noun (subject b) and place on line 7.
5. Write two adjectives describing subject b. Place on line 6.
6. Write three participles for subject b. Place on line 5.
7. Write four nouns on line 4. The first two should describe subject a. The second two should describe subject b.
8. Glue your peri-graph to a piece of blue or green construction paper and display!

Math

Transform refrigerator and stove boxes into a model of the Nautilus! Before constructing, discuss dimensions, ratios and relative sizes. Explain nautical speed (knots) before students make a speedometer for the ship. Students should understand temperature and weather before making thermometers and barometers for the ship.

Ask: Why would a submarine crew need to know about weather conditions? Discuss aquatic measurements (fathoms, leagues, etc.) and how submarines withstand being crushed by the weight and pressure of water.

Ask students to plot the course of the Nautilus on a map using longitude and latitude.

Music

Discuss sea chanteys with the class. Ask: What is the purpose of chanteys? What do they tell us about life at sea? Visit your library and borrow recordings of chanteys! One favorite is "Blow the Man Down." Ask students to write a sea chantey Captain Nemo might have sung.

Art

The sea provides unlimited opportunities for artistic expression. Display student-made realistic depictions of colorful ocean plants and animals on bulletin boards in the classroom. They can be made of poster board, construction paper, wooden utensils, plastic containers, etc. Each bulletin board becomes a different habitat, such as the sandy beach, tropical waters, the coral reef, etc.

Scrimshaw is the art of carving designs into pieces of shell, ivory or bone. Sailors often carved walrus tusks and whale teeth. Scrimshaw can be traced to the late 18th century, but was most popular from 1830 to 1850.

Ask: Why was the art so popular among sailors? Why do you think many people would be angry if the art were revived today?

Have students mimic the scrimshaw process:
1. Pour plaster of Paris into clean half-pint sized milk cartons and allow to harden.
2. Peel cartons away from hardened plaster.
3. Smooth plaster surface with fine sandpaper.
4. Place plaster in the center of the paper. Trace the base. Then, without picking up the plaster block, lay it on its side and trace the side. Return the block to an upright position. Trace the remaining three sides of the plaster the same way.
5. Draw your design within the traced area with a pencil, then transfer design onto plaster and carve with a paper clip end.
6. Wipe plaster surface with a paper towel. Rub black paste shoe polish into carving with a cotton swab. Try to keep polish off rest of surface.
7. Remove excess polish with a paper towel. Try not to remove polish from carved area.
8. Lightly sand surface with sandpaper to remove unwanted polish, being careful not to remove design.
9. Wipe plaster with clean paper towel. Seal shoe polish onto design with a coat of clear fingernail polish.

MARGUERITE SAWYER